POEMS BY FAVORITE POETS IN LARGE PRINT

POEMS BY FAVORITE POETS IN LARGE PRINT

Lesle Lewis, editor

G.K.HALL &CO.
Boston, Massachusetts
1992

G.K. Hall Large Print Book Series.

Set in 16 pt. Plantin.

Library of Congress Cataloging-in-Publication Data

Poems by favorite poets in large print / Lesle Lewis, editor.
     p.   cm. —(G.K. Hall large print book series)
  ISBN 0-8161-5029-X
  1. English poetry. 2. American poetry. 3. Large type books.
I. Lewis, Lesle.
PR1175.P618 1992
821.008—dc20   91-31002

ACKNOWLEDGMENTS

The editor gratefully acknowledges permission to reproduce copyright poems in this book.

Elizabeth Bishop: "Sestina" and "One Art" reprinted by permission of Farrar, Straus and Giroux, Inc. publishers of *The Complete Poems: 1927–1979* Copyright © 1979, 1983 by Alice Helen Methfessel.

Anne Bradstreet: "A Letter to Her Husband, Absent upon Public Employment" and "Here Follows Some Verses upon the Burning of Our House July 10th, 1666" reprinted by permission of the publishers from *The Works of Anne Bradstreet*, Jeannine Hensley, ed., Cambridge, Mass.: The Belknap Press of Harvard University Press, Copyright © 1967 by the President and Fellows of Harvard College.

Emily Brontë: "Long Neglect Has Worn Away", "Riches I Hold in Light Esteem" and "Stanzas" reprinted from *The Complete Poems of Emily Brontë*, Hatfield, ed. Columbia University Press.

CONTENTS

INTRODUCTION

I believe in the power of poetry to both comfort and inspire. When sound, metaphor and original combinations of words join together in a poem, new ways of understanding become possible. What was mundane or even incomprehensible is suddenly transformed into something deeply meaningful. Wordsworth's "bliss of solitude" for instance, is quite different from loneliness and conjures up a vision of ecstasy. In Yeats' "The Dawn" words are put together to remind us that being "ignorant and wanton as the dawn" is a blessing; Yeats reminds us of our innocence. And great poets like Elizabeth Bishop remind us to be proud of our own courage; "The art of losing isn't hard to master". The possibilities for insight are tremendous. It has been an exciting process to select these poems for large print readers.

Lovers of poetry come to know how they can enjoy the sounds and images of a poem without being able to verbalize the "meaning" of a poem. Great poets make music with their combinations of image and sound: "But he who kisses the joy as it flies/ Lives in eternity's sun rise." (Blake) "Rowing in Eden—/ Ah, the Sea!/ Might I but moor— Tonight—/ In Thee!" (Dickinson) Readers will bring their own interpretations to these poems. Every poem will speak differently to every reader.

For the convenience of the reader the poems have been grouped by poet in chronological order beginning with William Shakespeare (1564–1616) and ending with Robert Lowell (1917–1977). Many excellent and well-known poems will not be found in this collection because they have appeared in previous G.K. Hall large print anthologies. *Favorite Poems in Large Print* and *Best-Loved Poems in Large Print*, both edited by Virginia S. Reiser, are complete and inspiring anthologies.

Many people have helped me with the selection process. I want to thank Louise Forbush, Audrey Gilman Benson, Lois Adams Leach, Sally Lewis, Katherine Cushman, Laurie Cohen and William Doreski for their suggestions and contributions, and I'd also like to thank Shelley Roth for her help and support.

Lesle Lewis

Poems by
William
Shakespeare

Hark! Hark! the Lark
(from "Cymbeline")

Hark, hark! the lark at heaven's gate sings,
  And Phoebus gins arise,
His steeds to water at those springs
  On chalic'd flowers that lies;
And winking Mary-buds begin
  To ope their golden eyes.
With every thing that pretty is,
  My lady sweet, arise:
    Arise, arise!

Under the Greenwood Tree
(from "As You Like It")

Under the greenwood tree
Who loves to lie with me,
And turn his merry note
Unto the sweet bird's throat,
Come hither, come hither, come hither:
  Here shall he see
  No enemy
But winter and rough weather.

  Who doth ambition shun
  And loves to live i' the sun,

3

Seeking the food he eats,
And pleased with what he gets,
Come hither, come hither, come hither:
Here shall he see
No enemy
But winter and rough weather.

Two Loves I Have (Sonnet 144)

Two loves I have of comfort and despair,
Which like two spirits do suggest me still:
The better angel is a man right fair,
The worser spirit a woman, colored ill.
To win me soon to hell, my female evil
Tempteth my better angel from my side,
And would corrupt my saint to be a devil,
Wooing his purity with her foul pride.
And whether that my angel be turned fiend
Suspect I may, yet not directly tell;
But being both from me, both to each friend,
I guess one angel in another's hell.
Yet this shall I ne'er know, but live in doubt,
Till my bad angel fire my good one out.

When, in Disgrace (Sonnet 29)

When, in disgrace with fortune and men's eyes,
I all alone beweep my outcast state,
And trouble deaf heaven with my bootless cries,
And look upon myself, and curse my fate,

4

Wishing me like to one more rich in hope,
Featured like him, like him with friends
    possessed,
Desiring this man's art and that man's scope,
With what I most enjoy contented least;
Yet in these thoughts myself almost despising,
Haply I think on thee—and then my state,
Like to the lark at break of day arising
From sullen earth, sings hymns at heaven's
    gate;
For thy sweet love remembered such wealth
    brings
That then I scorn to change my state with
    kings.

When Daisies Pied
(from "Love's Labour's Lost")

SPRING

When daisies pied and violets blue
    And ladysmocks all silver-white
And cuckoobuds of yellow hue
    Do paint the meadows with delight,
The cuckoo then, on every tree,
Mocks married men; for thus sings he,
                    Cuckoo;
Cuckoo, cuckoo: Oh word of fear,
Unpleasing to a married ear!

When shepherds pipe on oaten straws,
    And merry larks are plowmen's clocks,

When turtles tread, and rooks, and daws,
   And maidens bleach their summer smocks,
The cuckoo then, on every tree,
Mocks married men; for thus sings he,
                       Cuckoo;
Cuckoo, cuckoo: Oh word of fear,
Unpleasing to a married ear!

WINTER

When icicles hang by the wall
   And Dick the shepherd blows his nail
And Tom bears logs into the hall,
   And milk comes frozen home in pail,
When blood is nipped and ways be foul,
Then nightly sings the staring owl,
                       Tu-who;
Tu-whit, tu-who: a merry note,
While greasy Joan doth keel the pot.

When all aloud the wind doth blow,
   And coughing drowns the parson's saw,
And birds sit brooding in the snow,
   And Marian's nose looks red and raw,
When roasted crabs hiss in the bowl,
Then nightly sings the staring owl,
                       Tu-who;
Tu-whit, tu-who: a merry note
While greasy Joan doth keel the pot.

Oh Mistress Mine
(from "Twelfth Night")

Oh mistress mine! where are you roaming?
Oh! stay and hear; your true love's coming,
   That can sing both high and low.
Trip no further, pretty sweeting;
Journeys end in lovers meeting,
   Every wise man's son doth know.

What is love? 'tis not hereafter;
Present mirth hath present laughter;
   What's to come is still unsure:

In delay there lies no plenty;
Then come kiss me, sweet and twenty,
   Youth's a stuff will not endure.

Poems by
John Donne

The Sun Rising

Busy old fool, unruly sun,
    Why dost thou thus,
Through windows, and through curtains call on
        us?
Must to thy motions lovers' seasons run?
    Saucy pedantic wretch, go chide
    Late school-boys, and sour prentices,
  Go tell court-huntsmen, that the King will
        ride,
  Call country ants to harvest offices;
Love, all alike, no season knows, nor clime,
Nor hours, days, months, which are the rags of
        time.

    Thy beams, so reverend, and strong
    Why shouldst thou think?
I could eclipse and cloud them with a wink,
But that I would not lose her sight so long:
    If her eyes have not blinded thine,
    Look, and tomorrow late, tell me,
  Whether both th'Indias of spice and mine
  Be where thou left'st them, or lie here with
        me.
Ask for those kings whom thou saw'st
        yesterday,
And thou shalt hear, All here in one bed lay.

She'is all states, and all princes, I,
  Nothing else is.
Princes do but play us; compared to this,
All honour's mimic; all wealth alchemy.
  Thou sun art half as happy as we,
  In that the world's contracted thus;
  Thine age asks ease, and since thy duties be
  To warm the world, that's done in warming
      us.
Shine here to us, and thou art everywhere;
This bed thy centre is, these walls, thy sphere.

Holy Sonnet #7

At the round earth's imagined corners, blow
Your trumpets, angels, and arise, arise
From death, you numberless infinities
Of souls, and to your scattered bodies go,
All whom the flood did, and fire shall
    o'erthrow,
All whom war, dearth, age, agues, tyrannies,
Despair, law, chance, hath slain, and you whose
    eyes,
Shall behold God, and never taste death's woe.
But let them sleep, Lord, and me mourn a space,
For, if above all these, my sins abound,
'Tis late to ask abundance of thy grace,
When we are there; here on this lowly ground,
Teach me how to repent; for that's as good
As if thou hadst sealed my pardon, with thy
    blood.

Holy Sonnet #9

If poisonous minerals, and if that tree,
Whose fruit threw death on else immortal us,
If lecherous goats, if serpents envious
Cannot be damned; alas, why should I be?
Why should intent or reason, born in me,
Make sins, else equal, in me more heinous?
And mercy being easy, and glorious
To God, in his stern wrath, why threatens he?
But who am I, that dare dispute with thee
O God? Oh! of thine only worthy blood,
And my tears, make a heavenly lethean flood,
And drown in it my sin's black memory;
That thou remember them, some claim as debt,
I think it mercy, if thou wilt forget.

Song

Sweetest love, I do not go,
    For weariness of thee,
Nor in hope the world can show
    A fitter love for me;
        But since that I
Must die at last, 'tis best,
To use my self in jest
    Thus by feigned deaths to die.

Yesternight the sun went hence,
    And yet is here today,
He hath no desire nor sense,

13

Nor half so short a way:
   Then fear not me,
But believe that I shall make
Speedier journeys, since I take
   More wings and spurs than he.

O how feeble is man's power,
   That if good fortune fall,
Cannot add another hour,
   Nor a lost hour recall!
     But come bad chance,
And we join to it our strength,
And we teach it art and length,
   Itself o'er us to advance.

When thou sigh'st, thou sigh'st not wind,
   But sigh'st my soul away,
When thou weep'st, unkindly kind,
   My life's blood doth decay.
     It cannot be
That thou lov'st me, as thou say'st,
If in thine my life thou waste,
   Thou art the best of me.

Let not thy divining heart
   Forethink me any ill,
Destiny may take thy part,
   And may thy fears fulfil;
     But think that we
Are but turned aside to sleep;
They who one another keep
   Alive, ne'er parted be.

Poems by
Ben Jonson

The Noble Nature

It is not growing like a tree
In bulk, doth make Man better be;
Or standing long an oak, three hundred year,
To fall a log at last, dry, bald, and sere:
    A lily of a day
    Is fairer far in May,
  Although it fall and die that night;
  It was the plant and flower of light.
In small proportions we just beauties see;
And in short measures, life may perfect be.

Song

Still to be neat, still to be drest,
As you were going to a feast;
Still to be pou'dred, still perfum'd:
Lady, it is to be presum'd,
Though arts hid causes are not found,
All is not sweet, all is not sound.

Give me a looke, give me a face,
That makes simplicitie a grace;
Robes loosely flowing, haire as free:
Such sweet neglect more taketh me,
Then all th'adulteries of art.
They strike mine eyes, but not my heart.

17

To Celia

Come my *Celia*, let us prove,
While we may, the sports of love;
Time will not be ours, for ever:
He, at length, our good will sever.
Spend not then his guifts in vaine.
Sunnes, that set, may rise againe:
But if once we loose this light,
'Tis, with us, perpetuall night.
Why should we deferre our joyes?
Fame, and rumor are but toyes.
Cannot we delude the eyes
Of a few poore houshold spyes?
Or his easier eares beguile,
So removed by our wile?

On My First Sonne

Farewell, thou child of my right hand, and joy;
  My sinne was too much hope of thee, lov'd
    boy,
Seven yeeres tho'wert lent to me, and I thee pay,
  Exacted by thy fate, on the just day.
O, could I loose all father now. For why
  Will man lament the state he should envie?
To have so soone scap'd worlds, and fleshes
    rage,
  And, if no other miserie, yet age?
Rest in soft peace, and, ask'd, say here doth lye
  Ben. Jonson his best piece of *poetrie*.

18

For whose sake, hence-forth, all his vowes be
   such,
   As what he loves may never like too much.

On My First Daughter

Here lyes to each her parents ruth,
Mary, the daughter of their youth:
Yet, all heavens gifts, being heavens due,
It makes the father, lesse, to rue.
At sixe moneths end, shee parted hence
With safetie of her innocence;
Whose soule heavens Queene, (whose name shee
   beares)
In comfort of her mothers teares,
Hath plac'd amongst her virgin-traine:
Where, while that sever'd doth remaine,
This grave partakes the fleshly birth.
Which cover lightly, gentle earth.

A Hymne to God
the Father

Heare mee, O God!
A broken heart,
Is my best part:
Use still thy rod,
   That I may prove
   Therein, thy Love.

If thou hadst not
   Beene sterne to mee,
   But left me free,
I had forgot
   My selfe and thee.

For, sin's so sweet,
   As minds ill bent
   Rarely repent,
Until they meet
   Their punishment.

Who more can crave
   Then thou hast done:
   That gav'st a Sonne,
To free a slave?
   First made of nought,
   Withall since bought.

Sinne, Death, and Hell,
   His glorious Name
   Quite overcame,
Yet I rebell,
   And slight the same.

But, I'le come in,
   Before my losse,
   Me farther tosse,
As sure to win
   Under his Crosse.

Poems by
Robert Herrick

The Primrose

    Aske me why I send you here
This sweet *Infanta* of the yeere?
    Aske me why I send to you
This Primrose, thus bepearl'd with dew?
    I will whisper to your eares,
The sweets of Love are mixt with tears.

    Ask me why this flower do's show
So yellow-green, and sickly too?
    Ask me why the stalk is weak
And bending, (yet it doth not break?)
    I will answer, These discover
What fainting hopes are in a Lover.

To Violets

1. Welcome Maids of Honour,
    You doe bring
    In the Spring;
  And wait upon her.

2. She has Virgins many,
    Fresh and faire;
    Yet you are
  More sweet then any.

3. Y'are the Maiden Posies,
    And so grac't,
    To be plac't,
  'Fore Damask Roses.

4. Yet though thus respected,
    By and by
    Ye doe lie,
  Poore Girles, neglected.

The White Island:
or Place of the Blest

In this world (the *Isle of Dreames*)
While we sit by sorrowes streames,
Teares and terrors are our theames
                Reciting:

But when once from hence we flie,
More and more approaching nigh
Unto young Eternitie
                Uniting:

In that *whiter Island*, where
Things are evermore sincere;
Candor here, and lustre there
                Delighting:

24

There no monstrous fancies shall
Out of hell an horrour call,
To create (or cause at all)
                    Affrighting.

There in calm and cooling sleep
We our eyes shall never steep;
But eternall watch shall keep,
                    Attending

Pleasures, such as shall pursue
Me immortaliz'd, and you;
And fresh joyes, as never too
                    Have ending.

Poems by
George Herbert

The Flower

How fresh, O Lord, how sweet and clean
Are thy returns! ev'n as the flowers in spring;
   To which, besides their own demean,
The late-past frosts tributes of pleasure bring.
            Grief melts away
            Like snow in May,
  As if there were no such cold thing.

Who would have thought my shrivel'd heart
Could have recover'd greennesse? It was gone
   Quite under ground; as flowers depart
To see their mother-root, when they have blown;
            Where they together
            All the hard weather,
  Dead to the world, keep house unknown.

These are thy wonders, Lord of power,
Killing and quickning, bringing down to hell
   And up to heaven in an houre;
Making a chiming of a passing-bell.
            We say amisse,
            This or that is:
  Thy word is all, if we could spell.

O that I once past changing were,
Fast in thy Paradise, where no flower can
   wither!

Many a spring I shoot up fair,
Offring at heav'n, growing and groning thither:
        Nor doth my flower
        Want a spring-showre,
My sinnes and I joining together.

But while I grow in a straight line,
Still upwards bent, as if heav'n were mine own,
   Thy anger comes, and I decline:
What frost to that? what pole is not the zone,
        Where all things burn,
        When thou dost turn,
And the least frown of thine is shown?

And now in age I bud again,
After so many deaths I live and write;
   I once more smell the dew and rain,
And relish versing: O my onely light,
        It cannot be
        That I am he
On whom thy tempests fell all night.

These are thy wonders, Lord of love,
To make us see we are but flowers that glide:
   Which when we once can finde and prove,
Thou hast a garden for us, where to bide.
        Who would be more,
        Swelling through store,
Forfeit their Paradise by their pride.

Love (III)

Love bade me welcome: yet my soul drew back,
            Guiltie of dust and sinne.
But quick-ey'd Love, observing me grow slack
            From my first entrance in,
Drew nearer to me, sweetly questioning,
            If I lack'd any thing.

A guest, I answer'd, worthy to be here:
            Love said, You shall be he.
I the unkinde, ungratefull? Ah my deare,
            I cannot look on thee.
Love took my hand, and smiling did reply,
            Who made the eyes but I?

Truth Lord, but I have marr'd them: let my
  shame
            Go where it doth deserve.
And know you not, sayes Love, who bore the
  blame?
            My deare, then I will serve.
You must sit down, sayes Love, and taste my
  meat:
            So I did sit and eat.

The Temper (I)

How should I praise thee, Lord! how should my
    rymes
  Gladly engrave thy love in steel,
  If what my soul doth feel sometimes,
    My soul might ever feel!

Although there were some fourtie heav'ns, or
    more,
  Sometimes I peere above them all;
  Sometimes I hardly reach a score,
    Sometimes to hell I fall.

O rack me not to such a vast extent;
  Those distances belong to thee:
  The world's too little for thy tent,
    A grave too big for me.

Wilt thou meet arms with man, that thou dost
    stretch
  A crumme of dust from heav'n to hell?
  Will great God measure with a wretch?
    Shall he thy stature spell?

O let me, when thy roof my soul hath hid,
  O let me roost and nestle there:
  Then of a sinner thou art rid,
    And I of hope and fear.

Yet take thy way; for sure thy way is best:
    Stretch or contract me, thy poore debter:
    This is but tuning of my breast,
        To make the musick better.

Whether I flie with angels, fall with dust,
    Thy hands made both, and I am there:
    Thy power and love, my love and trust
        Make one place ev'ry where.

Poems by
Thomas Carew

Disdain Returned

He that loves a rosy cheek,
  Or a coral lip admires,
Or from starlike eyes doth seek
  Fuel to maintain his fires;
As old Time makes these decay,
So his flames must waste away.

But a smooth and steadfast mind,
  Gentle thoughts, and calm desires,
Hearts with equal love combined,
  Kindle never-dying fires:—
Where these are not, I despise
Lovely cheeks or lips or eyes. . . .

The Spring

Now that the winter's gone, the earth hath lost
Her snow-white robes, and now no more the
  frost
Candies the grass, or casts an icy cream
Upon the silver lake or crystal stream;
But the warm sun thaws the benumbéd earth
And makes it tender, gives a sacred birth
To the dead swallow, wakes in hollow tree
The drowsy cuckoo and the humble bee.
Now do a choir of chirping minstrels bring

In triumph to the world the youthful spring.
The valleys, hills, and woods in rich array
Welcome the coming of the long'd-for May.
Now all things smile: only my love doth lour,
Nor hath the scalding noonday sun the power
To melt that marble ice which still doth hold
Her heart congeal'd, and makes her pity cold.
The ox, which lately did for shelter fly
Into the stall, doth now securely lie
In open fields; and love no more is made
By the fireside, but in the cooler shade:
Amyntas now doth with his Chloris sleep
Under a sycamore, and all things keep
Time with the season. Only she doth carry
June in her eyes, in her heart January.

Mediocrity in Love Rejected

Give me more love, or more disdain;
  The torrid or the frozen zone
Bring equal ease unto my pain;
  The temperate affords me none:
Either extreme, of love or hate,
Is sweeter than a calm estate.

Give me a storm; if it be love,
  Like Danaë in that golden shower,
I swim in pleasure; if it prove
  Disdain, that torrent will devour
My vulture hopes; and he's possessed

Of heaven that's but from hell released.
    Then crown my joys, or cure my pain;
    Give me more love or more disdain.

Poems by
John Milton

Song: On *May* Morning

Now the bright morning Star, Dayes harbinger,
Comes dancing from the East, and leads with
    her
The Flowry *May,* who from her green lap
    throws
The yellow Cowslip, and the pale Primrose.
  Hail bounteous *May* that dost inspire
  Mirth and youth, and warm desire,
  Woods and Groves are of thy dressing,
  Hill and Dale doth boast thy blessing.
Thus we salute thee with our early Song,
And welcom thee, and wish thee long.

How Soon Hath Time
(Sonnet 7)

How soon hath Time the suttle theef of youth,
  Stoln on his wing my three and twentith
    yeer!
  My hasting dayes fly on with full career,
  But my late spring no bud or blossom
    shew'th.
Perhaps my semblance might deceave the truth
  That I to manhood am arriv'd so neer,
  And inward ripenes doth much less appear,
  That som more timely-happy spirits indu'th.

43

Yet be it less or more, or soon or slow,
 It shall be still in strictest measure eev'n
 To that same lot, however mean or high,
Toward which Time leads me, and the will of
  Heav'n;
 All is, if I have grace to use it so,
 As ever in my great task-maisters eye.

When Faith and Love
(Sonnet 14)

When Faith and Love which parted from thee
  never,
 Had rip'n'd thy just soul to dwell with God,
 Meekly thou didst resigne this earthy load
Of death, call'd life; which us from life doth
  sever.
Thy Works and Almes, and all thy good
  Endeavor
 Staid not behind, nor in the grave were trod;
 But as Faith pointed with her golden rod,
Follow'd thee up to joy and bliss for ever.
Love led them on, and Faith who knew them
  best
 Thy handmaids, clad them o're with purple
  beames
And azure wings, that up they flew so drest,
And spake the truth of thee in glorious theames
 Before the Judge, who thenceforth bidd thee
  rest,
 And drink thy fill of pure immortal streames.

Poems by
Anne Bradstreet

A Letter to Her Husband, Absent Upon Public Employment

My head, my heart, mine eyes, my life, nay,
  more,
My joy, my magazine of earthly store,
If two be one, as surely thou and I,
How stayest thou there, whilst I at Ipswich lie?
So many steps, head from the heart to sever,
If but a neck, soon should we be together.
I, like the Earth this season, mourn in black,
My Sun is gone so far in's zodiac,
Whom whilst I 'joyed, nor storms, nor frost I
  felt,
His warmth such frigid colds did cause to melt.
My chilled limbs now numbed lie forlorn;
Return, return, sweet Sol, from Capricorn;
In this dead time, alas, what can I more
Than view those fruits which through thy heat I
  bore?
Which sweet contentment yield me for a space,
True living pictures of their father's face.
O strange effect! now thou art southward gone,
I weary grow the tedious day so long;
But when thou northward to me shalt return,
I wish my Sun may never set, but burn
Within the Cancer of my glowing breast,
The welcome house of him my dearest guest.

Where ever, ever stay, and go not thence,
Till nature's sad decree shall call thee hence;
Flesh of thy flesh, bone of thy bone,
I here, thou there, yet both but one.

Here Follows Some Verses Upon the Burning of Our House July 10th, 1666. Copied Out of a Loose Paper

In silent night when rest I took
For sorrow near I did not look
I wakened was with thund'ring noise
And piteous shrieks of dreadful voice.
That fearful sound of "Fire!" and "Fire!"
Let no man know is my desire.
I, starting up, the light did spy,
And to my God my heart did cry
To strengthen me in my distress
And not to leave me succorless.
Then, coming out, beheld a space
The flame consume my dwelling place.
And when I could no longer look,
I blest His name that gave and took,
That laid my goods now in the dust.
Yea, so it was, and so 'twas just.
It was His own, it was not mine,
Far be it that I should repine;
He might of all justly bereft
But yet sufficient for us left.

When by the ruins oft I past
My sorrowing eyes aside did cast,
And here and there the places spy
Where oft I sat and long did lie:
Here stood that trunk, and there that chest,
There lay that store I counted best.
My pleasant things in ashes lie,
And them behold no more shall I.

Under thy roof no guest shall sit,
Nor at thy table eat a bit.
No pleasant tale shall e'er be told,
Nor things recounted done of old.
No candle e'er shall shine in thee,
Nor bridegroom's voice e'er heard shall be.
In silence ever shall thou lie,
Adieu, Adieu, all's vanity.
Then straight I 'gin my heart to chide,
And did thy wealth on earth abide?
Didst fix thy hope on mold'ring dust?
The arm of flesh didst make thy trust?
Raise up thy thoughts above the sky
That dunghill mists away may fly.
Thou hast an house on high erect,
Framed by that mighty Architect,
With glory richly furnished,
Stands permanent though this be fled.
It's purchased and paid for too
By Him who hath enough to do.
A price so vast as is unknown
Yet by His gift is made thine own;
There's wealth enough, I need no more,

Farewell, my pelf, farewell my store.
The world no longer let me love,
My hope and treasure lies above.

Poems by
Andrew Marvell

Eyes and Tears

1
How wisely Nature did decree,
With the same eyes to weep and see!
That, having viewed the object vain,
We might be ready to complain.

2
Thus since the self-deluding sight,
In a false angle takes each height,
These tears, which better measure all,
Like watery lines and plummets fall.

3
Two tears, which Sorrow long did weigh
Within the scales of either eye,
And then paid out in equal poise,
Are the true price of all my joys.

4
What in the world most fair appears,
Yea, even laughter, turns to tears:
And all the jewels which we prize,
Melt in these pendants of the eyes.

5
I have through every garden been,
Amongst the red, the white, the green,

And yet, from all the flowers I saw,
No honey but these tears, could draw.

6
So the all-seeing sun each day
Distills the world with chemic ray,
But finds the essence only show'rs,
Which straight in pity back he pours.

7
Yet happy they whom grief doth bless,
That weep the more, and see the less:
And, to preserve their sight more true,
Bathe still their eyes in their own dew.

8
So Magdalen, in tears more wise
Dissolved those captivating eyes,
Whose liquid chains could flowing meet
To fetter her Redeemer's feet.

9
Not full sails hasting loaden home,
Nor the chaste lady's pregnant womb,
Nor Cynthia teeming shows so fair,
As two eyes swoll'n with weeping are.

10
The sparkling glance that shoots desire,
Drenched in these waves does lose its fire.
Yea, oft the Thunderer pity takes
And here the hissing lightning slakes.

11

The incense was to heaven dear,
Not as a perfume, but a tear.
And stars show lovely in the night,
But as they seem the tears of light.

12

Ope then, mine eyes, your double sluice,
And practise so your noblest use;
For others too can see, or sleep,
But only human eyes can weep.

13

Now, like two clouds dissolving, drop,
And at each tear in distance stop:
Now, like two fountains, trickle down;
Now, like two floods o'erturn and drown.

14

Thus let your streams o'erflow your springs,
Till eyes and tears be the same things:
And each the other's difference bears;
These weeping eyes, those seeing tears.

On a Drop of Dew

See how the orient dew,
Shed from the bosom of the morn
   Into the blowing roses,
Yet careless of its mansion new,
For the clear region where 'twas born

Round in itself incloses:
And in its little globe's extent,
Frames as it can its native element.
How it the purple flow'r does slight,
Scarce touching where it lies,
But gazing back upon the skies,
Shines with a mournful light,
Like its own tear,
Because so long divided from the sphere.
Restless it rolls and unsecure,
Trembling lest it grow impure,
Till the warm sun pity its pain,
And to the skies exhale it back again.
So the soul, that drop, that ray
Of the clear fountain of eternal day,
Could it within the human flow'r be seen,
Remembering still its former height,
Shuns the sweet leaves and blossoms green,
And recollecting its own light,
Does, in its pure and circling thoughts, express
The greater heaven in an heaven less.
In how coy a figure wound,
Every way it turns away:
So the world excluding round,
Yet receiving in the day,
Dark beneath, but brought above,
Here disdaining, there in love.
How loose and easy hence to go,
How girt and ready to ascend,
Moving but on a point below,
It all about does upwards bend.
Such did the manna's sacred dew distill,

White and entire, though congealed and chill,
Congealed on earth: but does, dissolving, run
Into the glories of th' almighty sun.

The Mower Against Gardens

Luxurious man, to bring his vice in use,
    Did after him the world seduce,
And from the fields the flowers and plants
        allure,
    Where nature was most plain and pure.
He first enclosed within the gardens square
    A dead and standing pool of air,
And a more luscious earth for them did knead,
    Which stupified them while it fed.
The pink grew then as double as his mind;
    The nutriment did change the kind.
With strange perfumes he did the roses taint,
    And flowers themselves were taught to paint.
The tulip, white, did for complexion seek,
    And learned to interline its cheek:
Its onion root they then so high did hold,
    That one was for a meadow sold.
Another world was searched, through oceans
        new,
    To find the *Marvel of Peru.*
And yet these rarities might be allowed
    To man, that sovereign thing and proud,
Had he not dealt between the bark and tree,
    Forbidden mixtures there to see.

No plant now knew the stock from which it
    came;
  He grafts upon the wild the tame:
That th' uncertain and adulterate fruit
  Might put the palate in dispute.
His green seraglio has its eunuchs too,
  Lest any tyrant him outdo.
And in the cherry he does nature vex,
  To procreate without a sex.
'Tis all enforced, the fountain and the grot,
  While the sweet fields do lie forgot:
Where willing nature does to all dispense
  A wild and fragrant innocence:
And fauns and fairies do the meadows till,
  More by their presence than their skill.
Their statues, polished by some ancient hand,
  May to adorn the gardens stand:
But howsoe'er the figures do excel,
  The gods themselves with us do dwell.

The Mower's Song

1

  My mind was once the true survey
  Of all these meadows fresh and gay,
  And in the greenness of the grass
  Did see its hopes as in a glass;
  When Juliana came, and she
What I do to the grass, does to my thoughts
    and me.

2

    But these, while I with sorrow pine,
    Grew more luxuriant still and fine,
    That not one blade of grass you spied,
    But had a flower on either side;
    When Juliana came, and she
What I do to the grass, does to my thoughts
      and me.

3

    Unthankful meadows, could you so
    A fellowship so true forgo,
    And in your gaudy May-games meet,
    While I lay trodden under feet?
    When Juliana came, and she
What I do to the grass, does to my thoughts
      and me.

4

    But what you in compassion ought,
    Shall now by my revenge be wrought:
    And flow'rs, and grass, and I and all,
    Will in one common ruin fall.
    For Juliana comes, and she
What I do to the grass, does to my thoughts
      and me.

5

    And thus, ye meadows, which have been
    Companions of my thoughts more green,
    Shall now the heraldry become

With which I will adorn my tomb;
  For Juliana comes, and she
What I do to the grass, does to my thoughts
    and me.

Poems by
William Blake

Songs of Innocence

Introduction

Piping down the valleys wild
Piping songs of pleasant glee
On a cloud I saw a child,
And he laughing said to me:

"Pipe a song about a Lamb."
So I piped with merry chear.
"Piper pipe that song again—"
So I piped, he wept to hear.

"Drop thy pipe thy happy pipe,
Sing thy songs of happy chear."
So I sung the same again
While he wept with joy to hear.

"Piper sit thee down and write
In a book that all may read—"
So he vanish'd from my sight.
And I pluck'd a hollow reed,

And I made a rural pen,
And I stain'd the water clear,
And I wrote my happy songs
Every child may joy to hear.

63

The Shepherd

How sweet is the Shepherd's sweet lot,
From the morn to the evening he strays:
He shall follow his sheep all the day
And his tongue shall be filled with praise.

For he hears the lambs' innocent call,
And he hears the ewes' tender reply,
He is watchful while they are in peace,
For they know when their Shepherd is nigh.

Eternity

He who binds to himself a joy
Does the wingéd life destroy
But he who kisses the joy as it flies
Lives in eternity's sun rise.

The Divine Image

To Mercy, Pity, Peace, and Love,
All pray in their distress:
And to these virtues of delight
Return their thankfulness.

For Mercy, Pity, Peace, and Love,
Is God, our father dear:
And Mercy, Pity, Peace, and Love,
Is Man, his child and care.

For Mercy has a human heart,
Pity, a human face:
And Love, the human form divine,
And Peace, the human dress.

Then every man of every clime,
That prays in his distress,
Prays to the human form divine,
Love, Mercy, Pity, Peace.

And all must love the human form,
In heathen, Turk, or Jew.
Where Mercy, Love, & Pity dwell,
There God is dwelling too.

Ah Sun-flower

Ah Sun-flower! weary of time,
Who countest the steps of the Sun,
Seeking after that sweet golden clime
Where the traveller's journey is done;

Where the Youth pined away with desire,
And the pale Virgin shrouded in snow,
Arise from their graves and aspire,
Where my Sun-flower wishes to go.

Poems by
Robert Burns

Green Grow the Rashes

Green grow the rashes, O;
   Green grow the rashes, O;
The sweetest hours that e'er I spend,
   Are spent amang the lasses, O!

There's nought but care on ev'ry han',
   In ev'ry hour that passes, O:
What signifies the life o' man,
   An' 'twere na for the lasses, O.
                    (*Chorus*)

The warly race may riches chase,
   An' riches still may fly them, O;
An' though at last they catch them fast,
   Their hearts can ne'er enjoy them, O.
                    (*Chorus*)

But gie me a canny hour at e'en,
   My arms about my dearie, O;
An' warly cares, an' warly men,
   May a' gae tapsalteerie, O!
                    (*Chorus*)

For you sae douce, ye sneer at this,
   Ye're nought but senseless asses, O:

The wisest man the warl' saw,
   He dearly loved the lasses, O.
                    (*Chorus*)

Auld nature swears, the lovely dears
   Her noblest work she classes, O:
Her prentice han' she tried on man,
   An' then she made the lasses, O.
                    (*Chorus*)

John Anderson, My Jo[1]

John Anderson my jo, John,
   When we were first acquent,
Your locks were like the raven,
   Your bonie brow was brent;
But now your brow is beld, John,
   Your locks are like the snow;
But blessings on your frosty pow,
   John Anderson, my jo.

John Anderson my jo, John,
   We clamb the hill thegither;
And mony a canty day, John,
   We've had wi' ane anither:
Now we maun totter down, John,
   And hand in hand we'll go,
And sleep thegither at the foot,
   John Anderson, my jo.

[1]jo—joy

Poems by *William Wordsworth*

Written in March

WHILE RESTING ON THE BRIDGE AT THE FOOT
OF BROTHER'S WATER

The cock is crowing,
The stream is flowing,
The small birds twitter,
The lake doth glitter,
The green field sleeps in the sun;
The oldest and youngest
Are at work with the strongest;
The cattle are grazing,
Their heads never raising;
There are forty feeding like one!

Like an army defeated
The Snow hath retreated,
And now doth fare ill
On the top of the bare hill;
The Plough-boy is whooping—anon—anon:
There's joy in the mountains;
There's life in the fountains;
Small clouds are sailing,
Blue sky prevailing;
The rain is over and gone!

So Fair, So Sweet, Withal So Sensitive

So fair, so sweet, withal so sensitive,
Would that the little Flowers were born to live,
Conscious of half the pleasure which they give;

That to this mountain-daisy's self were known
The beauty of its star-shaped shadow, thrown
On the smooth surface of this naked stone!

And what if hence a bold desire should mount
High as the Sun, that he could take account
Of all that issues from his glorious fount!

So might he ken how by his sovereign aid
These delicate companionships are made;
And how he rules the pomp of light and shade;

And were the Sister-power that shines by night
So privileged, what a countenance of delight
Would through the clouds break forth on
    human sight!

Fond fancies! wheresoe'er shall turn thine eye
On earth, air, ocean, or the starry sky,
Converse with Nature in pure sympathy;

All vain desires, all lawless wishes quelled,
Be Thou to love and praise alike impelled,
Whatever boon is granted or withheld.

Nutting

———————————————It seems a day,
(I speak of one from many singled out)
One of those heavenly days which cannot die,
When forth I sallied from our cottage-door,
And with a wallet o'er my shoulder slung,
A nutting crook in hand, I turn'd my steps
Towards the distant woods, a Figure quaint,
Trick'd out in proud disguise of Beggar's weeds
Put on for that occasion, by advice
And exhortation of my frugal Dame.
Motley accoutrement! of power to smile
At thorns, and brakes, and brambles, and, in
   truth,
More ragged than need was. Among the woods,
And o'er the pathless rocks, I forc'd my way
Until, at length, I came to one dear nook
Unvisited, where not a broken bough
Droop'd with its wither'd leaves, ungracious
   sign
Of devastation, but the hazels rose
Tall and erect, with milk-white clusters hung,
A virgin scene!—A little while I stood,
Breathing with such suppression of the heart
As joy delights in; and with wise restraint
Voluptuous, fearless of a rival, eyed
The banquet, or beneath the trees I sate
Among the flowers, and with the flowers I
   play'd;
A temper known to those, who, after long
And weary expectation, have been bless'd

With sudden happiness beyond all hope.—
—Perhaps it was a bower beneath whose leaves
The violets of five seasons re-appear
And fade, unseen by any human eye,
Where fairy water-breaks do murmur on
For ever, and I saw the sparkling foam,
And with my cheek on one of those green
   stones
That, fleec'd with moss, beneath the shady
   trees,
Lay round me scatter'd like a flock of sheep,
I heard the murmur and the murmuring sound,
In that sweet mood when pleasure loves to pay
Tribute to ease, and, of its joy secure,
The heart luxuriates with indifferent things,
Wasting its kindliness on stocks and stones,
And on the vacant air. Then up I rose,
And dragg'd to earth both branch and bough,
   with crash
And merciless ravage; and the shady nook
Of hazels, and the green and mossy bower
Deform'd and sullied, patiently gave up
Their quiet being: and unless I now
Confound my present feelings with the past,
Even then, when from the bower I turn'd away,
Exulting, rich beyond the wealth of kings,
I felt a sense of pain when I beheld
The silent trees and the intruding sky.—

Then, dearest Maiden! move along these shades
In gentleness of heart with gentle hand
Touch,—for there is a Spirit in the woods.

76

Surprised by Joy

Surprised by joy—impatient as the Wind
I turned to share the transport—Oh! with
   whom
But thee, deep buried in the silent tomb,
That spot which no vicissitude can find?
Love, faithful love, recalled thee to my mind—
But how could I forget thee? Through what
   power,
Even for the least division of an hour,
Have I been so beguiled as to be blind
To my most grievous loss!—That thought's
   return
Was the worst pang that sorrow ever bore,
Save one, one only, when I stood forlorn,
Knowing my heart's best treasure was no more;
That neither present time, nor years unborn
Could to my sight that heavenly face restore.

Poems by
Sir Walter Scott

From "Lady of the Lake"

Harp of the North, farewell! The hills grow
    dark,
    On purple peaks a deeper shade descending;
In twilight copse the glow-worm lights her
    spark,
    The deer, half-seen, are to the covert
    wending.
Resume thy wizard elm! the fountain lending,
    And the wild breeze, thy wilder minstrelsy;
Thy numbers sweet with nature's vespers
    blending,
    With distant echo from the fold and lea,
And herd-boy's evening pipe, and hum of
    housing bee.

Yet, once again, farewell, thou Minstrel Harp!
    Yet, once again, forgive my feeble sway,
And little reck I of the censure sharp
    May idly cavil at an idle lay.
Much have I owed thy strains on life's long
    way,
    Through secret woes the world has never
    known,
When on the weary night dawned wearier day,
    And bitterer was the grief devoured alone.—
That I o'erlive such woes, Enchantress! is
    thine own.

Hark! as my lingering footsteps slow retire,
    Some Spirit of the Air has waked thy string!
'T is now a seraph bold, with touch of fire,
    'T is now the brush of Fairy's frolic wing.
Receding now, the dying numbers ring
    Fainter and fainter down the rugged dell;
And now the mountain breezes scarcely bring
    A wandering witch-note of the distant spell—
And now, 't is silent all!—Enchantress, fare
    thee well!

County Guy
From *Quentin Durward*

Ah! County Guy, the hour is nigh,
    The sun has left the lea,
The orange flower perfumes the bower,
    The breeze is on the sea.
The lark his lay who thrilled all day
    Sits hushed his partner nigh;
Breeze, bird, and flower confess the hour,
    But where is County Guy?

The village maid steals through the shade,
    Her shepherd's suit to hear;
To beauty shy by lattice high,
    Sings high-born Cavalier.
The star of Love, all stars above,
    Now reigns o'er earth and sky;
And high and low the influence know—
    But where is County Guy?

Poems by
Samuel Taylor Coleridge

From "The Rime of
the Ancient Mariner"

Farewell, farewell! but this I tell
To thee, thou Wedding Guest!
He prayeth well, who loveth well
Both man and bird and beast.

He prayeth best, who loveth best
All things both great and small;
For the dear God who loveth us,
He made and loveth all.

The Mariner, whose eye is bright,
Whose beard with age is hoar,
Is gone: and now the Wedding Guest
Turned from the bridegroom's door.

He went like one that hath been stunned,
And is of sense forlorn:
A sadder and a wiser man,
He rose the morrow morn.

Time, Real and Imaginary

AN ALLEGORY

On the wide level of a mountain's head,
(I knew not where, but 'twas some faery
      place)
Their pinions, ostrich-like, for sails out-spread,
Two lovely children run an endless race,
    A sister and a brother!
    This far outstripp'd the other;
  Yet ever runs she with reverted face,
  And looks and listens for the boy behind:
    For he, alas! is blind!
O'er rough and smooth with even step he
      passed,
And knows not whether he be first or last.

Work Without Hope

LINES COMPOSED 21ST FEBRUARY 1825

All Nature seems at work. Slugs leave their lair—
The bees are stirring—birds are on the wing—
And Winter slumbering in the open air
Wears on his smiling face a dream of Spring!
And I the while, the sole unbusy thing,
Nor honey make, nor pair, nor build, nor
    sing.

Yet well I ken the banks where amaranths
  blow,
Have traced the fount whence streams of nectar
  flow.
Bloom, O ye amaranths! bloom for whom ye
  may,
For me ye bloom not! Glide, rich streams,
  away!
With lips unbrightened, wreathless brow, I
  stroll:
And would you learn the spells that drowse my
  soul?
Work without Hope draws nectar in a sieve,
And Hope without an object cannot live.

Frost at Midnight

The Frost performs its secret ministry,
Unhelped by any wind. The owlet's cry
Came loud—and hark, again! loud as before.
The inmates of my cottage, all at rest,
Have left me to that solitude, which suits
Abstruser musings: save that at my side
My cradled infant slumbers peacefully.
'Tis calm indeed! so calm, that it disturbs
And vexes meditation with its strange
And extreme silentness. Sea, hill, and wood,
This populous village! Sea, and hill, and wood,
With all the numberless goings-on of life,
Inaudible as dreams! the thin blue flame
Lies on my low-burnt fire, and quivers not;

Only that film, which fluttered on the grate,
Still flutters there, the sole unquiet thing.
Methinks its motion in this hush of nature
Gives it dim sympathies with me who live,
Making it a companionable form,
Whose puny flaps and freaks the idling Spirit
By its own moods interprets, everywhere
Echo or mirror seeking of itself,
And makes a toy of Thought.

                              But O! how oft,
How oft, at school, with most believing mind,
Presageful, have I gazed upon the bars,
To watch that fluttering *stranger!* and as oft
With unclosed lids, already had I dreamt
Of my sweet birthplace, and the old church
    tower,
Whose bells, the poor man's only music, rang
From morn to evening, all the hot Fair-day,
So sweetly, that they stirred and haunted me
With a wild pleasure, falling on mine ear
Most like articulate sounds of things to come!
So gazed I, till the soothing things, I dreamt,
Lulled me to sleep, and sleep prolonged my
    dreams!
And so I brooded all the following morn,
Awed by the stern preceptor's face, mine eye
Fixed with mock study on my swimming book:
Save if the door half opened, and I snatched
A hasty glance, and still my heart leaped up,
For still I hoped to see the *stranger's* face,

Townsman, or aunt, or sister more beloved,
My playmate when we both were clothed alike!

Dear Babe, that sleepest cradled by my side,
Whose gentle breathings, heard in this deep
   calm,
Fill up the interspersèd vacancies
And momentary pauses of the thought!
My babe so beautiful! it thrills my heart
With tender gladness, thus to look at thee,
And think that thou shalt learn far other lore,
And in far other scenes! For I was reared
In the great city, pent 'mid cloisters dim,
And saw nought lovely but the sky and stars.
But *thou*, my babe! shalt wander like a breeze
By lakes and sandy shores, beneath the crags
Of ancient mountain, and beneath the clouds,
Which image in their bulk both lakes and
   shores
And mountain crags: so shalt thou see and hear
The lovely shapes and sounds intelligible
Of that eternal language, which thy God
Utters, who from eternity doth teach
Himself in all, and all things in himself.
Great universal Teacher! he shall mold
Thy spirit, and by giving make it ask.

Therefore all seasons shall be sweet to thee,
Whether the summer clothe the general earth
With greenness, or the redbreast sit and sing
Betwixt the tufts of snow on the bare branch
Of mossy apple tree, while the nigh thatch

Smokes in the sun-thaw; whether the eave-drops fall
Heard only in the trances of the blast,
Or if the secret ministry of frost
Shall hang them up in silent icicles,
Quietly shining to the quiet Moon.

Cologne

In Köhln, a town of monks and bones,
And pavements fang'd with murderous stones
And rags, and hags, and hideous wenches;
I counted two and seventy stenches,
All well defined, and several stinks!
Ye Nymphs that reign o'er sewers and sinks,
The river Rhine, it is well known,
Doth wash your city of Cologne;
But tell me, Nymphs, what power divine
Shall henceforth wash the river Rhine?

Epitaph

Stop, Christian passer-by!—Stop, child of God,
And read with gentle breast. Beneath this sod
A poet lies, or that which once seemed he.
O lift one thought in prayer for S. T. C.;
That he who many a year with toil of breath
Found death in life, may here find life in death!
Mercy for praise—to be forgiven for fame
He asked, and hoped, through Christ. Do thou
    the same!

90

Poems by
George Gordon, Lord Byron

Stanzas for Music

1

There be none of Beauty's daughters
   With a magic like thee;
And like music on the waters
   Is thy sweet voice to me:
When, as if its sound were causing
The charméd ocean's pausing,
The waves lie still and gleaming,
And the lulled winds seem dreaming;

2

And the midnight moon is weaving
   Her bright chain o'er the deep;
Whose breast is gently heaving,
   As an infant's asleep:
So the spirit bows before thee,
To listen and adore thee;
With a full but soft emotion,
Like the swell of summer's ocean.

Stanzas

WHEN A MAN HATH NO FREEDOM
TO FIGHT FOR AT HOME

When a man hath no freedom to fight for at
    home,
  Let him combat for that of his neighbors;
Let him think of the glories of Greece and of
    Rome,
  And get knocked on his head for his labors.

To do good to mankind is the chivalrous
    plan,
  And is always as nobly requited;
Then battle for freedom wherever you can,
  And, if not shot or hanged, you'll get
    knighted.

Stanzas
Written on the road between
Florence and Pisa

O talk not to me of a name great in story;
The days of our youth are the days of our glory;
And the myrtle and ivy of sweet two-and-twenty
Are worth all your laurels, though ever so
  plenty.

94

What are garlands and crowns to the brow that
    is wrinkled?
Tis but as a dead flower with May-dew be-
    sprinkled:
Then away with all such from the head that is
    hoary—
What care I for the wreaths that can only give
    glory?

Oh Fame!—if I e'er took delight in thy praises,
'Twas less for the sake of thy high-sounding
    phrases,
Than to see the bright eyes of the dear one
    discover
She thought that I was not unworthy to love
    her.

There chiefly I sought thee, there only I found
    thee;
Her glance was the best of the rays that
    surround thee;
When it sparkled o'er aught that was bright in
    my story,
I knew it was love, and I felt it was glory.

Poems by
Percy Bysshe Shelley

To ———

Music, when soft voices die,
Vibrates in the memory—
Odors, when sweet violets sicken,
Live within the sense they quicken.
Rose leaves, when the rose is dead,
Are heaped for the belovéd's bed;
And so thy thoughts, when thou art gone,
Love itself shall slumber on.

To Jane: The Keen Stars
Were Twinkling

1
The keen stars were twinkling,
And the fair moon was rising among them,
 Dear Jane!
The guitar was tinkling,
But the notes were not sweet till you sung them
 Again.

2
As the moon's soft splendor
O'er the faint cold starlight of Heaven
 Is thrown,

99

So your voice most tender
To the strings without soul had then given
    Its own.

    3

The stars will awaken,
Though the moon sleep a full hour later,
    Tonight;
  No leaf will be shaken
Whilst the dews of your melody scatter
    Delight.

    4

Though the sound overpowers,
Sing again, with your dear voice revealing
    A tone
Of some world far from ours,
Where music and moonlight and feeling
    Are one.

Mutability

    1

The flower that smiles today
    Tomorrow dies;
All that we wish to stay,
    Tempts and then flies.
What is this world's delight?
Lightning that mocks the night,
    Brief even as bright.

2

Virtue, how frail it is!
    Friendship how rare!
Love, how it sells poor bliss
    For proud despair!
But we, though soon they fall,
Survive their joy and all
    Which ours we call.

3

Whilst skies are blue and bright,
    Whilst flowers are gay,
Whilst eyes that change ere night
    Make glad the day,
Whilst yet the calm hours creep,
Dream thou—and from thy sleep
    Then wake to weep.

Song

Rarely, rarely comest thou,
    Spirit of Delight!
Wherefore hast thou left me now
    Many a day and night?
Many a weary night and day
'Tis since thou art fled away.

How shall ever one like me
    Win thee back again?
With the joyous and the free
    Thou wilt scoff at pain.

Spirit false! thou hast forgot
All but those who need thee not.

As a lizard with the shade
    Of a trembling leaf,
Thou with sorrow art dismayed;
    Even the sighs of grief
Reproach thee, that thou art not near,
And reproach thou wilt not hear.

Let me set my mournful ditty
    To a merry measure:
Thou wilt never come for pity—
    Thou wilt come for pleasure;
Pity then will cut away
Those cruel wings, and thou wilt stay.—

I love all that thou lovest,
    Spirit of Delight!
The fresh Earth in new leaves drest,
    And the starry night,
Autumn evening, and the morn
When the golden mists are born.

I love snow, and all the forms
    Of the radiant frost;
I love waves and winds and storms—
    Every thing almost
Which is Nature's and may be
Untainted by man's misery.

I love tranquil Solitude,
   And such society
As is quiet, wise and good;
   Between thee and me
What difference? but thou dost possess
The things I seek—not love them less.

I love Love—though he has wings,
   And like light can flee—
But above all other things,
   Spirit, I love thee—
Thou art Love and Life! O come,
Make once more my heart thy home.

To Wordsworth

Poet of Nature, thou hast wept to know
   That things depart which never may return;
   Childhood and youth, friendship and love's
      first glow,
   Have fled like sweet dreams, leaving thee to
      mourn.
These common woes I feel. One loss is mine,
   Which thou too feel'st, yet I alone deplore;
   Thou wert as a lone star whose light did shine
   On some frail bark in winter's midnight roar;
Thou hast like to a rock-built refuge stood
   Above the blind and battling multitude;
   In honored poverty thy voice did weave
Songs consecrate to truth and liberty;—

Deserting these, thou leavest me to grieve,
Thus having been, that thou shouldst cease to
  be.

Poems by
John Keats

What the Thrush Said

O thou whose face hath felt the Winter's wind,
Whose eye has seen the snow-clouds hung in
  mist,
And the black elm tops 'mong the freezing
  stars,
To thee the spring will be a harvest-time.
O thou, whose only book has been the light
Of supreme darkness which thou feddest on
Night after night when Phœbus was away,
To thee the Spring shall be a triple morn.
O fret not after knowledge—I have none,
And yet my song comes native with the
  warmth.
O fret not after knowledge—I have none,
And yet the Evening listens. He who saddens
At thought of idleness cannot be idle,
And he's awake who thinks himself asleep.

Ode to Psyche

O Goddess! hear these tuneless numbers, wrung
  By sweet enforcement and remembrance dear,
And pardon that thy secrets should be sung
  Even into thine own soft-conchéd ear;
Surely I dreamt today, or did I see
  The wingéd Psyche with awakened eyes?

I wandered in a forest thoughtlessly,
   And, on the sudden, fainting with surprise,
Saw two fair creatures, couchéd side by side
    In deepest grass, beneath the whisp'ring roof
    Of leaves and trembled blossoms, where there
       ran
     A brooklet, scarce espied:

'Mid hushed, cool-rooted flowers, fragrant-eyed,
   Blue, silver-white, and budded Tyrian,
They lay calm-breathing on the bedded grass;
    Their arms embracéd, and their pinions too;
    Their lips touched not, but had not bade
      adieu,
As if disjoinéd by soft-handed slumber,
And ready still past kisses to outnumber
    At tender eye-dawn of aurorean love:
     The wingéd boy I knew;
    But who wast thou, O happy, happy dove?
     His Psyche true!

O latest born and loveliest vision far
   Of all Olympus' faded hierarchy!
Fairer than Phoebe's sapphire-regioned star,
   Or Vesper; amorous glowworm of the sky;
Fairer than these, though temple thou hast
     none,
    Nor altar heaped with flowers;
Nor virgin choir to make delicious moan
    Upon the midnight hours;
No voice, no lute, no pipe, no incense sweet
   From chain-swung censer teeming;

No shrine, no grove, no oracle, no heat
　　Of pale-mouthed prophet dreaming.

O brightest! though too late for antique vows,
　　Too, too late for the fond believing lyre,
When holy were the haunted forest boughs,
　　Holy the air, the water, and the fire;
Yet even in these days so far retired
　　From happy pieties, thy lucent fans,
　　Fluttering among the faint Olympians,
I see, and sing, by my own eyes inspired.
So let me be thy choir, and make a moan
　　　Upon the midnight hours;
Thy voice, thy lute, thy pipe, thy incense sweet
　　From swingéd censer teeming;
Thy shrine, thy grove, thy oracle, thy heat
　　Of pale-mouthed prophet dreaming.

Yes, I will be thy priest, and build a fane
　　In some untrodden region of my mind,
Where branchéd thoughts, new grown with
　　　　pleasant pain,
　　Instead of pines shall murmur in the wind:
Far, far around shall those dark-clustered trees
　　Fledge the wild-ridgéd mountains steep by
　　　　steep;
And there by zephyrs, streams, and birds, and
　　　bees,
　　The moss-lain Dryads shall be lulled to sleep;
And in the midst of this wide quietness
A rosy sanctuary will I dress
With the wreathed trellis of a working brain,

With buds, and bells, and stars without a
    name,
With all the gardener Fancy e'er could feign,
  Who breeding flowers, will never breed the
    same:
And there shall be for thee all soft delight
  That shadowy thought can win,
A bright torch, and a casement ope at night,
  To let the warm Love in!

Stanzas

In a drear-nighted December,
    Too happy, happy tree,
Thy branches ne'er remember
    Their green felicity:
  The north cannot undo them,
  With a sleety whistle through them;
  Nor frozen thawings glue them
    From budding at the prime.

In a drear-nighted December,
    Too happy, happy brook,
Thy bubblings ne'er remember
    Apollo's summer look;
  But with a sweet forgetting,
  They stay their crystal fretting,
  Never, never petting
    About the frozen time.

Ah! would 't were so with many
    A gentle girl and boy!
But were there ever any
    Writh'd not at passèd joy?
To know the change and feel it,
When there is none to heal it,
Nor numbèd sense to steal it,
    Was never said in rhyme.

The Eve of St. Agnes

1

St. Agnes' Eve—Ah, bitter chill it was!
The owl, for all his feathers, was a-cold;
The hare limped trembling through the
    frozen grass,
And silent was the flock in woolly fold:
Numb were the Beadsman's fingers, while he
    told
His rosary, and while his frosted breath,
Like pious incense from a censer old,
Seemed taking flight for heaven, without a
    death,
Past the sweet Virgin's picture, while his prayer
    he saith.

2

His prayer he saith, this patient, holy man;
Then takes his lamp, and riseth from his
    knees,
And back returneth, meager, barefoot, wan,

Along the chapel aisle by slow degrees:
The sculptured dead, on each side, seem to
    freeze,
Imprisoned in black, purgatorial rails:
Knights, ladies, praying in dumb orat'ries,
He passeth by; and his weak spirit fails
To think how they may ache in icy hoods and
    mails.

3

Northward he turneth through a little door,
And scarce three steps, ere Music's golden
    tongue
Flattered to tears this aged man and poor;
But no—already had his deathbell rung:
The joys of all his life were said and sung:
His was harsh penance on St. Agnes' Eve:
Another way he went, and soon among
Rough ashes sat he for his soul's reprieve,
And all night kept awake, for sinner's sake to
    grieve.

4

That ancient Beadsman heard the prelude
    soft;
And so it chanced, for many a door was wide,
From hurry to and fro. Soon, up aloft,
The silver, snarling trumpets 'gan to chide:
The level chambers, ready with their pride,
Were glowing to receive a thousand guests:
The carvéd angels, ever eager-eyed,

Stared, where upon their heads the cornice
    rests,
With hair blown back, and wings put crosswise
    on their breasts.

     5
At length burst in the argent revelry,
With plume, tiara, and all rich array,
Numerous as shadows haunting faerily
The brain, new stuffed, in youth, with
    triumphs gay
Of old romance. These let us wish away,
And turn, sole-thoughted, to one Lady there,
Whose heart had brooded, all that wintry
    day;
On love, and winged St. Agnes' saintly care,
As she had heard old dames full many times
    declare.

     6
They told her how, upon St. Agnes' Eve,
Young virgins might have visions of delight,
And soft adorings from their loves receive
Upon the honeyed middle of the night,
If ceremonies due they did aright;
As, supperless to bed they must retire,
And couch supine their beauties, lily white;
Nor look behind, nor sideways, but require
Of Heaven with upward eyes for all that they
    desire.

7

Full of this whim was thoughtful Madeline:
The music, yearning like a God in pain,
She scarcely heard: her maiden eyes divine,
Fixed on the floor, saw many a sweeping
    train
Pass by—she heeded not at all: in vain
Came many a tiptoe, amorous cavalier,
And back retired; not cooled by high disdain;
But she saw not: her heart was otherwhere:
She sighed for Agnes' dreams, the sweetest of
    the year.

8

She danced along with vague, regardless eyes,
Anxious her lips, her breathing quick and
    short:
The hallowed hour was near at hand: she
    sighs
Amid the timbrels, and the thronged resort
Of whisperers in anger, or in sport;
'Mid looks of love, defiance, hate, and scorn,
Hoodwinked with faery fancy; all amort,
Save to St. Agnes and her lambs unshorn,
And all the bliss to be before tomorrow morn.

9

So, purposing each moment to retire,
She lingered still. Meantime, across the
    moors,
Had come young Porphyro, with heart on fire
For Madeline. Beside the portal doors,

Buttressed from moonlight, stands he, and
    implores
All saints to give him sight of Madeline,
But for one moment in the tedious hours,
That he might gaze and worship all
    unseen;
Perchance speak, kneel, touch, kiss—in sooth
    such things have been.

10

He ventures in: let no buzzed whisper tell:
All eyes be muffled, or a hundred swords
Will storm his heart, Love's fev'rous
    citadel:
For him, those chambers held barbarian
    hordes,
Hyena foemen, and hot-blooded lords,
Whose very dogs would execrations howl
Against his lineage: not one breast affords
Him any mercy, in that mansion foul,
Save one old beldame, weak in body and in
    soul.

11

Ah, happy chance! the aged creature came,
Shuffling along with ivory-headed wand,
To where he stood, hid from the torch's
    flame,
Behind a broad hall-pillar, far beyond
The sound of merriment and chorus bland:
He startled her; but soon she knew his face,
And grasped his fingers in her palsied hand,

Saying, "Mercy, Porphyro! hie thee from this
   place;
They are all here tonight, the whole
   bloodthirsty race!

   12
"Get hence! get hence! there's dwarfish
   Hildebrand;
He had a fever late, and in the fit
He curséd thee and thine, both house and
   land:
Then there's that old Lord Maurice, not a
   whit
More tame for his gray hairs—Alas me! flit!
Flit like a ghost away."—"Ah, Gossip dear,
We're safe enough; here in this armchair sit,
And tell me how"—"Good Saints! not here,
   not here;
Follow me, child, or else these stones will be
   thy bier."

   13
He followed through a lowly archéd way,
Brushing the cobwebs with his lofty plume,
And as she muttered "Well-a—well-a-day!"
He found him in a little moonlight room,
Pale, latticed, chill, and silent as a tomb.
"Now tell me where is Madeline," said he,
"O tell me, Angela, by the holy loom
Which none but secret sisterhood may see,
When they St. Agnes' wool are weaving
   piously."

14

"St Agnes! Ah! it is St. Agnes' Eve—
Yet men will murder upon holy days:
Thou must hold water in a witch's sieve,
And be liege lord of all the Elves and Fays,
To venture so: it fills me with amaze
To see thee, Porphyro!—St. Agnes' Eve!
God's help! my lady fair the conjuror plays
This very night: good angels her deceive!
But let me laugh awhile, I've mickle time to
    grieve."

15

Feebly she laugheth in the languid moon,
While Porphyro upon her face doth look,
Like puzzled urchin on an aged crone
Who keepeth closed a wondrous riddle-book,
As spectacled she sits in chimney nook.
But soon his eyes grew brilliant, when she
    told
His lady's purpose; and he scarce could brook
Tears, at the thought of those enchantments
    cold,
And Madeline asleep in lap of legends old.

16

Sudden a thought came like a full-blown rose,
Flushing his brow, and in his painéd heart
Made purple riot: then doth he propose
A stratagem, that makes the beldame start:
"A cruel man and impious thou art:

Sweet lady, let her pray, and sleep, and
   dream
Alone with her good angels, far apart
From wicked men like thee. Go, go!—I deem
Thou canst not surely be the same that thou
   didst seem."

17

"I will not harm her, by all saints I swear,"
Quoth Porphyro: "O may I ne'er find grace
When my weak voice shall whisper its last
   prayer,
If one of her soft ringlets I displace,
Or look with ruffian passion in her face:
Good Angela, believe me by these tears;
Or I will, even in a moment's space,
Awake, with horrid shout, my foemen's ears,
And beard them, though they be more fanged
   than wolves and bears."

18

"Ah! why wilt thou affright a feeble soul?
A poor, weak, palsy-stricken, churchyard
   thing,
Whose passing bell may ere the midnight toll;
Whose prayers for thee, each morn and
   evening,
Were never missed."—Thus plaining, doth
   she bring
A gentler speech from burning Porphyro;
So woeful and of such deep sorrowing,

That Angela gives promise she will do
Whatever he shall wish, betide her weal or woe.

19

Which was, to lead him, in close secrecy,
Even to Madeline's chamber, and there hide
Him in a closet, of such privacy
That he might see her beauty unespied,
And win perhaps that night a peerless bride,
While legioned faeries paced the coverlet,
And pale enchantment held her sleepy-eyed.
Never on such a night have lovers met,
Since Merlin paid his Demon all the monstrous
    debt.

20

"It shall be as thou wishest," said the Dame:
"All cates and dainties shall be storéd there
Quickly on this feast night: by the tambour
    frame
Her own lute thou wilt see: no time to spare,
For I am slow and feeble, and scarce dare
On such a catering trust my dizzy head.
Wait here, my child, with patience; kneel in
    prayer
The while: Ah! thou must needs the lady wed,
Or may I never leave my grave among the
    dead."

21

So saying, she hobbled off with busy fear.
The lover's endless minutes slowly passed:

The dame returned, and whispered in his ear
To follow her; with aged eyes aghast
From fright of dim espial. Safe at last,
Through many a dusky gallery, they gain
The maiden's chamber, silken, hushed, and
    chaste;
Where Porphyro took covert, pleased amain.
His poor guide hurried back with agues in her
    brain.

22

Her falt'ring hand upon the balustrade,
Old Angela was feeling for the stair,
When Madeline, St. Agnes' charméd maid,
Rose, like a missioned spirit, unaware:
With silver taper's light, and pious care,
She turned, and down the aged gossip led
To a safe level matting. Now prepare,
Young Porphyro, for gazing on that bed;
She comes, she comes again, like ringdove
    frayed and fled.

23

Out went the taper as she hurried in;
Its little smoke, in pallid moonshine, died:
She closed the door, she panted, all akin
To spirits of the air, and visions wide:
No uttered syllable, or, woe betide!
But to her heart, her heart was voluble,
Paining with eloquence her balmy side;

120

As though a tongueless nightingale should
    swell
Her throat in vain, and die, heart-stifled, in her
    dell.

24

A casement high and triple-arched there was,
All garlanded with carven imag'ries
Of fruits, and flowers, and bunches of knot-
    grass,
And diamonded with panes of quaint device,
Innumerable of stains and splendid dyes,
As are the tiger-moth's deep-damasked wings;
And in the midst, 'mong thousand heraldries,
And twilight saints, and dim emblazonings,
A shielded scutcheon blushed with blood of
    queens and kings.

25

Full on this casement shone the wintry moon,
And threw warm gules on Madeline's fair
    breast,
As down she knelt for heaven's grace and
    boon;
Rose-bloom fell on her hands, together
    pressed,
And on her silver cross soft amethyst,
And on her hair a glory, like a saint:
She seemed a splendid angel, newly dressed,
Save wings, for heaven—Porphyro grew faint:
She knelt, so pure a thing, so free from mortal
    taint.

26

Anon his heart revives: her vespers done,
Of all its wreathéd pearls her hair she frees;
Unclasps her warméd jewels one by one;
Loosens her fragrant bodice; by degrees
Her rich attire creeps rustling to her knees:
Half-hidden, like a mermaid in sea-weed,
Pensive awhile she dreams awake, and sees,
In fancy, fair St. Agnes in her bed,
But dares not look behind, or all the charm is
    fled.

27

Soon, trembling in her soft and chilly nest,
In sort of wakeful swoon, perplexed she lay,
Until the poppied warmth of sleep oppressed
Her soothéd limbs, and soul fatigued away;
Flown, like a thought, until the morrow-day;
Blissfully havened both from joy and pain;
Clasped like a missal where swart Paynims
    pray;
Blinded alike from sunshine and from rain,
As though a rose should shut, and be a bud
    again.

28

Stol'n to this paradise, and so entranced,
Porphyro gazed upon her empty dress,
And listened to her breathing, if it chanced
To wake into a slumberous tenderness;
Which when he heard, that minute did he
    bless,

And breathed himself: then from the closet
    crept,
Noiseless as fear in a wide wilderness,
And over the hushed carpet, silent, stepped,
And 'tween the curtains peeped, where, lo!—
    how fast she slept.

29

Then by the bedside, where the faded moon
Made a dim, silver twilight, soft he set
A table, and, half anguished, threw thereon
A cloth of woven crimson, gold, and jet—
O for some drowsy Morphean amulet!
The boisterous, midnight, festive clarion,
The kettledrum, and far-heard clarinet,
Affray his ears, though but in dying tone—
The hall door shuts again, and all the noise is
    gone.

30

And still she slept an azure-lidded sleep,
In blanchéd linen, smooth, and lavendered,
While he from forth the closet brought a heap
Of candied apple, quince, and plum, and
    gourd;
With jellies soother than the creamy curd,
And lucent syrups, tinct with cinnamon;
Manna and dates, in argosy transferred
From Fez; and spicéd dainties, every one,
From silken Samarcand to cedared Lebanon.

31

These delicates he heaped with glowing hand
On golden dishes and in baskets bright
Of wreathéd silver: sumptuous they stand
In the retiréd quiet of the night,
Filling the chilly room with perfume light.—
"And now, my love, my seraph fair, awake!
Thou art my heaven, and I thine eremite:
Open thine eyes, for meek St. Agnes' sake,
Or I shall drowse beside thee, so my soul doth
    ache."

32

Thus whispering, his warm, unnervéd arm
Sank in her pillow. Shaded was her dream
By the dusk curtains: 'twas a midnight charm
Impossible to melt as icéd stream:
The lustrous salvers in the moonlight gleam;
Broad golden fringe upon the carpet lies:
It seemed he never, never could redeem
From such a steadfast spell his lady's eyes;
So mused awhile, entoiled in wooféd fantasies.

33

Awakening up, he took her hollow lute—
Tumultuous—and, in chords that tenderest
    be,
He played an ancient ditty, long since mute,
In Provence called "*La belle dame sans merci*"
Close to her ear touching the melody;
Wherewith disturbed, she uttered a soft
    moan:

He ceased—she panted quick—and suddenly
Her blue affrayéd eyes wide open shone:
Upon his knees he sank, pale as smooth-
    sculptured stone.

34

Her eyes were open, but she still beheld,
Now wide awake, the vision of her sleep:
There was a painful change, that nigh
    expelled
The blisses of her dream so pure and deep,
At which fair Madeline began to weep,
And moan forth witless words with many a
    sigh;
While still her gaze on Porphyro would keep,
Who knelt, with joinéd hands and piteous eye,
Fearing to move or speak, she looked so
    dreamingly.

35

"Ah, Porphyro!" said she, "but even now
Thy voice was at sweet tremble in mine ear,
Made tunable with every sweetest vow;
And those sad eyes were spiritual and clear:
How changed thou art! how pallid, chill, and
    drear!
Give me that voice again, my Porphyro,
Those looks immortal, those complainings
    dear!

Oh leave me not in this eternal woe,
For if thou diest, my Love, I know not where
   to go."

   36
Beyond a mortal man impassioned far
At these voluptuous accents, he arose,
Ethereal, flushed, and like a throbbing star
Seen mid the sapphire heaven's deep repose;
Into her dream he melted, as the rose
Blendeth its odor with the violet—
Solution sweet: meantime the frost-wind
   blows
Like Love's alarum pattering the sharp sleet
Against the windowpanes; St. Agnes' moon hath
   set.

   37
'Tis dark: quick pattereth the flaw-blown
   sleet:
"This is no dream, my bride, my Madeline!"
'Tis dark: the icéd gusts still rave and beat:
"No dream, alas! alas! and woe is mine!
Porphyro will leave me here to fade and pine.—
Cruel! what traitor could thee hither bring?
I curse not, for my heart is lost in thine,
Though thou forsakest a deceivéd thing—
A dove forlorn and lost with sick unprunéd wing."

   38
"My Madeline! sweet dreamer! lovely bride!
Say, may I be for aye thy vassal blest?

Thy beauty's shield, heart-shaped and vermeil
   dyed?
Ah, silver shrine, here will I take my rest
After so many hours of toil and quest,
A famished pilgrim—saved by miracle.
Though I have found, I will not rob thy nest
Saving of thy sweet self; if thou think'st well
To trust, fair Madeline, to no rude infidel.

39

"Hark! 'tis an elfin-storm from faery land,
Of haggard seeming, but a boon indeed:
Arise—arise! the morning is at hand—
The bloated wassaillers will never heed—
Let us away, my love, with happy speed;
There are no ears to hear, or eyes to see—
Drowned all in Rhenish and the sleepy mead:
Awake! arise! my love, and fearless be,
For o'er the southern moors I have a home for
   thee."

40

She hurried at his words, beset with fears,
For there were sleeping dragons all around,
At glaring watch, perhaps, with ready spears—
Down the wide stairs a darkling way they
   found.—
In all the house was heard no human sound.
A chain-dropped lamp was flickering by each
   door;
The arras, rich with horseman, hawk, and
   hound,

Fluttered in the besieging wind's uproar;
And the long carpets rose along the gusty floor.

41

They glide, like phantoms, into the wide hall;
Like phantoms, to the iron porch, they glide;
Where lay the Porter, in uneasy sprawl,
With a huge empty flagon by his side:
The wakeful bloodhound rose, and shook his
    hide,
But his sagacious eye an inmate owns:
By one, and one, the bolts full easy slide:
The chains lie silent on the footworn stones;
The key turns, and the door upon its hinges
    groans.

42

And they are gone: aye, ages long ago
These lovers fled away into the storm.
That night the Baron dreamt of many a woe,
And all his warrior-guests, with shade and
    form
Of witch, and demon, and large coffin-worm,
Were long be-nightmared. Angela the old
Died palsy-twitched, with meager face
    deform;
The Beadsman, after thousand aves told,
For aye unsought for slept among his ashes
    cold.

To Solitude

O Solitude! if I must with thee dwell,
  Let it not be among the jumbled heap
  Of murky buildings; climb with me the
      steep,—
Nature's observatory—whence the dell,
Its flowery slopes, its river's crystal swell,
  May seem a span; let me thy vigils keep
  'Mongst boughs pavillion'd, where the deer's
    swift leap
Startles the wild bee from the fox-glove bell.
But though I'll gladly trace these scenes with
      thee,
  Yet the sweet converse of an innocent mind,
Whose words are images of thoughts refin'd,
  Is my soul's pleasure; and it sure must be
Almost the highest bliss of human-kind,
  When to thy haunts two kindred spirits flee.

Poems by
Ralph Waldo Emerson

The Rhodora

In May, when sea-winds pierced our solitudes,
I found the fresh Rhodora in the woods,
Spreading its leafless blooms in a damp nook,
To please the desert and the sluggish brook.
The purple petals, fallen in the pool,
Made the black water with their beauty gay;
Here might the red-bird come his plumes to
  cool,
And court the flower that cheapens his array.
Rhodora! if the sages ask thee why
This charm is wasted on the earth and sky,
Tell them, dear, that if eyes were made for
  seeing,
Then Beauty is its own excuse for being:
Why thou wert there, O rival of the rose!
I never thought to ask, I never knew;
But, in my simple ignorance, suppose
The self-same Power that brought me there
  brought you.

Good-bye

Good-bye, proud world! I'm going home:
Thou art not my friend, and I'm not thine.
Long through thy weary crowds I roam;
A river-ark on the ocean brine,
Long I've been tossed like the driven foam;
But now, proud world! I'm going home.

Good-bye to Flattery's fawning face;
To Grandeur with his wise grimace;
To upstart Wealth's averted eye;
To supple Office, low and high;
To crowded halls, to court and street;
To frozen hearts and hasting feet;
To those who go, and those who come;
Good-bye, proud world! I'm going home.

I am going to my own hearth-stone,
Bosomed in yon green hills alone,—
A secret nook in a pleasant land,
Whose groves the frolic fairies planned;
Where arches green, the livelong day,
Echo the blackbird's roundelay,
And vulgar feet have never trod
A spot that is sacred to thought and God.

O, when I am safe in my sylvan home,
I tread on the pride of Greece and Rome;
And when I am stretched beneath the pines,
Where the evening star so holy shines,
I laugh at the lore and the pride of man,

At the sophist schools, and the learned clan;
For what are they all, in their high conceit,
When man in the bush with God may meet?

The World-Soul

Thanks to the morning light,
   Thanks to the foaming sea,
To the uplands of New-Hampshire,
   To the green-haired forest free;
Thanks to each man of courage,
   To the maids of holy mind;
To the boy with his games undaunted,
   Who never looks behind.

Cities of proud hotels,
   Houses of rich and great,
Vice nestles in your chambers,
   Beneath your roofs of slate.
It cannot conquer folly,
   Time-and-space-conquering steam,
And the light-outspeeding telegraph
   Bears nothing on its beam.

The politics are base;
   The letters do not cheer;
And 't is far in the deeps of history,
   The voice that speaketh clear.
Trade and the streets ensnare us,
   Our bodies are weak and worn;

We plot and corrupt each other,
    And we despoil the unborn.

Yet there in the parlour sits
    Some figure of noble guise,—
Our angel, in a stranger's form,
    Or woman's pleading eyes;
Or only a flashing sunbeam
    In at the window-pane;
Or Music pours on mortals
    Its beautiful disdain.

The inevitable morning
    Finds them who in cellars be;
And be sure the all-loving Nature
    Will smile in a factory.
Yon ridge of purple landscape,
    Yon sky between the walls,
Hold all the hidden wonders,
    In scanty intervals.

Alas! the Sprite that haunts us
    Deceives our rash desire;
It whispers of the glorious gods,
    And leaves us in the mire.
We cannot learn the cipher
    That's writ upon our cell;
Stars help us by a mystery
    Which we could never spell.

If but one hero knew it,
    The world would blush in flame;

The sage, till he hit the secret,
  Would hang his head for shame.
But our brothers have not read it,
  Not one has found the key;
And henceforth we are comforted,—
  We are but such as they.

Still, still the secret presses;
  The nearing clouds draw down;
The crimson morning flames into
  The fopperies of the town.
Within, without the idle earth,
  Stars weave eternal rings;
The sun himself shines heartily,
  And shares the joy he brings.

And what if Trade sow cities
  Like shells along the shore,
And thatch with towns the prairie
    broad,
  With railways ironed o'er?—
They are but sailing foam-bells
  Along Thought's causing stream,
And take their shape and sun-colour
  From him that sends the dream.

For Destiny does not like
  To yield to men the helm;
And shoots his thought, by hidden
    nerves,
  Throughout the solid realm.
The patient Daemon sits,

With roses and a shroud;
He has his way, and deals his gifts,—
  But ours is not allowed.

He is no churl nor trifler,
  And his viceroy is none,—
Love-without-weakness,—
  Of Genius sire and son.
And his will is not thwarted;
  The seeds of land and sea
Are the atoms of his body bright,
  And his behest obey.

He serveth the servant,
  The brave he loves amain;
He kills the cripple and the sick,
  And straight begins again.
For gods delight in gods,
  And thrust the weak aside;
To him who scorns their charities,
  Their arms fly open wide.

When the old world is sterile,
  And the ages are effete,
He will from wrecks and sediment
  The fairer world complete.
He forbids to despair;
  His cheeks mantle with mirth;
And the unimagined good of men
  Is yeaning at the birth.

Spring still makes spring in the mind,
    When sixty years are told;
Love wakes anew this throbbing heart,
    And we are never old.
Over the winter glaciers,
    I see the summer glow,
And, through the wild-piled snowdrift,
    The warm rosebuds below.

Brahma

If the red slayer think he slays,
    Or if the slain think he is slain,
They know not well the subtle ways
    I keep, and pass, and turn again.

Far or forgot to me is near;
    Shadow and sunlight are the same;
The vanished gods to me appear;
    And one to me are shame and fame.

They reckon ill who leave me out;
    When me they fly, I am the wings;
I am the doubter and the doubt,
    And I the hymn the Brahmin sings.

The strong gods pine for my abode,
    And pine in vain the sacred Seven,
But thou, meek lover of the good!
    Find me, and turn thy back on heaven.

Grace

How much, preventing God! how much I
  owe
To the defenses thou hast round me set:
Example, custom, fear, occasion slow,
These scornéd bondmen were my parapet.
I dare not peep over this parapet
To gauge with glance the roaring gulf below,
The depths of sin to which I had descended,
Had not these me against myself defended.

Poems by
Elizabeth Barrett Browning

From "A Woman's Shortcomings"

Unless you can muse in a crowd all day
   On the absent face that fixed you;
Unless you can love, as the angels may,
   With the breadth of heaven betwist you;
Unless you can dream that his faith is fast,
   Through behoving and unbehoving;
Unless you can *die* when the dream is past—
   Oh, never call it loving!

When Our Two Souls Stand Up
(Sonnet 22)

When our two souls stand up erect and strong,
Face to face, silent, drawing nigh and nigher,
Until the lengthening wings break into fire
At either curvèd point,—what bitter wrong
Can the earth do to us, that we should not long
Be here contented? Think. In mounting higher,
The angels would press on us and aspire
To drop some golden orb of perfect song
Into our deep, dear silence. Let us stay
Rather on earth, Belovèd,—where the unfit
Contrarious moods of men recoil away
And isolate pure spirits, and permit
A place to stand and love in for a day,
With darkness and the death-hour rounding it.

A Man's Requirements

I

Love me, Sweet, with all thou art,
  Feeling, thinking, seeing;
Love me in the lightest part,
  Love me in full being.

II

Love me with thine open youth
  In its frank surrender;
With the vowing of thy mouth.
  With its silence tender.

III

Love me with thine azure eyes,
  Made for earnest granting;
Taking color from the skies,
  Can Heaven's truth be wanting?

IV

Love me with their lids, that fall
  Snow-like at first meeting;
Love me with thine heart, that all
  Neighbors then see beating.

V

Love me with thine hand stretched out
  Freely—open-minded:
Love me with thy loitering foot,—
  Hearing one behind it.

VI

Love me with thy voice, that turns
   Sudden faint above me;
Love me with thy blush that burns
   When I murmur *Love me!*

VII

Love me with thy thinking soul,
   Break it to love-sighing;
Love me with thy thoughts that roll
   On through living—dying.

VIII

Love me in thy gorgeous airs,
   When the world has crowned thee;
Love me, kneeling at thy prayers,
   With the angels round thee.

IX

Love me pure, as musers do,
   Up the woodlands shady:
Love me gaily, fast and true,
   As a winsome lady.

X

Through all hopes that keep us brave,
   Farther off or nigher,
Love me for the house and grave,
   And for something higher.

XI

Thus, if thou wilt prove me, Dear,
  Woman's love no fable,
I will love *thee*—half a year—
  As a man is able.

From "Aurora Leigh"

Without considering whether they were fit
To do me good. Mark, there. We get no good
By being ungenerous, even to a book,
And calculating profits,—so much help
By so much reading. It is rather when
We gloriously forget ourselves and plunge
Soul-forward, headlong, into a book's profound,
Impassioned for its beauty and salt of truth—
'Tis then we get the right good from a book.

If Thou Must Love Me
(Sonnet 14)

If thou must love me, let it be for nought
Except for love's sake only. Do not say
'I love her for her smile—her look—her way
Of speaking gently,—for a trick of thought
That falls in well with mine, and certes brought
A sense of pleasant ease on such a day'—
For these things in themselves, Belovèd, may
Be changed, or change for thee,—and love, so
  wrought,

May be unwrought so. Neither love me for
Thine own dear pity's wiping my cheeks dry,—
A creature might forget to weep, who bore
Thy comfort long, and lose thy love thereby!
But love me for love's sake, that evermore
Thou mayst love on, through love's eternity.

Poems by
Henry Wadsworth Longfellow

The Arrow and the Song

I shot an arrow into the air,
It fell to earth, I knew not where;
For, so swiftly it flew, the sight
Could not follow it in its flight.

I breathed a song into the air,
It fell to earth, I knew not where;
For who has sight so keen and
  strong,
That it can follow the flight of song?

Long, long afterward, in an oak
I found the arrow, still unbroke;
And the song, from beginning to end,
I found again in the heart of a friend.

From "The Song of Hiawatha"

By the shores of Gitche Gumee,
By the shining Big-Sea-Water,
Stood the wigwam of Nokomis,
Daughter of the Moon, Nokomis.
Dark behind it rose the forest,
Rose the black and gloomy pine-trees,
Rose the firs with cones upon them;
Bright before it beat the water,

Beat the clear and sunny water,
Beat the shining Big-Sea-Water.
  There the wrinkled old Nokomis
Nursed the little Hiawatha,
Rocked him in his linden cradle,
Bedded soft in moss and rushes,
Safely bound with reindeer sinews;
Stilled his fretful wail by saying,
"Hush! the Naked Bear will hear thee!"
Lulled him into slumber, singing,
"Ewa-yea! my little owlet!
Who is this, that lights the wigwam?
With his great eyes lights the wigwam?
Ewa-yea! my little owlet!"
  Many things Nokomis taught him
Of the stars that shine in heaven;
Showed him Ishkoodah, the comet,
Ishkoodah, with fiery tresses;
Showed the Death-Dance of the spirits,
Warriors with their plumes and war-clubs,
Flaring far away to northward
In the frosty nights of Winter;
Showed the broad white road in heaven,
Pathway of the ghosts, the shadows.
Running straight across the heavens,
Crowded with the ghosts, the shadows.
  At the door on summer evenings
Sat the little Hiawatha;
Heard the whispering of the pine-trees,
Heard the lapping of the waters,
Sounds of music, words of wonder;
"Minne-wawa!" said the pine-trees,

"Mudway-aushka!" said the water.
    Saw the fire-fly, Wah-wah-taysee,
Flitting through the dusk of evening,
With the twinkle of its candle
Lighting up the brakes and bushes,
And he sang the song of children,
Sang the song Nokomis taught him:
"Wah-wah-taysee, little fire-fly,
Little, flitting, white-fire insect,
Little, dancing, white-fire creature,
Light me with your little candle,
Ere upon my bed I lay me,
Ere in sleep I close my eyelids!"
    Saw the moon rise from the water
Rippling, rounding from the water,
Saw the flecks and shadows on it,
Whispered, "What is that, Nokomis?"
And the good Nokomis answered:
"Once a warrior, very angry,
Seized his grandmother, and threw her
Up into the sky at midnight;
Right against the moon he threw her;
'Tis her body that you see there."
    Saw the rainbow in the heaven,
In the eastern sky, the rainbow,
Whispered, "What is that, Nokomis?"
And the good Nokomis answered:
"'T is the heaven of flowers you see there
All the wild-flowers of the forest,
All the lilies of the prairie,
When on earth they fade and perish,
Blossom in that heaven above us."

When he heard the owls at midnight,
Hooting, laughing in the forest,
"What is that?" he cried in terror,
"What is that," he said, "Nokomis?"
And the good Nokomis answered:
"That is but the owl and owlet,
Talking in their native language,
Talking, scolding at each other."
    Then the little Hiawatha
Learned of every bird its language,
Learned their names and all their secrets,
How they built their nests in Summer,
Where they hid themselves in Winter,
Talked with them whene'er he met them,
Called them "Hiawatha's Chickens."
    Of all beasts he learned the language,
Learned their names and all their secrets,
How the beavers built their lodges,
Where the squirrels hid their acorns,
How the reindeer ran so swiftly,
Why the rabbit was so timid,
Talked with them whene'er he met them,
Called them "Hiawatha's Brothers."

The Light of Stars

The night is come, but not too soon;
    And sinking silently,
All silently, the little moon
    Drops down behind the sky.

There is no light in earth or heaven
    But the cold light of stars;
And the first watch of night is given
    To the red planet Mars.

Is it the tender star of love?
    The star of love and dreams?
Oh no! from that blue tent above
    A hero's armor gleams.

And earnest thoughts within me rise,
    When I behold afar,
Suspended in the evening skies,
    The shield of that red star.

O star of strength! I see thee stand
    And smile upon my pain;
Thou beckonest with thy mailèd hand,
    And I am strong again.

Within my breast there is no light
    But the cold light of stars;
I give the first watch of the night
    To the red planet Mars.

The star of the unconquered will,
    He rises in my breast,
Serene, and resolute, and still,
    And calm, and self-possessed.

And thou, too, whosoe'er thou art,
    That readest this brief psalm,

As one by one thy hopes depart,
  Be resolute and calm.

Oh, fear not in a world like this,
  And thou shalt know erelong,
Know how sublime a thing it is
  To suffer and be strong.

The Builders

All are architects of Fate,
  Working in these walls of Time;
Some with massive deeds and great,
  Some with ornaments of rhyme.

Nothing useless is, or low;
  Each thing in its place is best;
And what seems but idle show
  Strengthens and supports the rest.

For the structure that we raise,
  Time is with materials filled;
Our to-days and yesterdays
  Are the blocks with which we build.

Truly shape and fashion these;
  Leave no yawning gaps between;
Think not, because no man sees,
  Such things will remain unseen.

In the elder days of Art,
    Builders wrought with greatest care
Each minute and unseen part;
    For the Gods see everywhere.

Let us do our work as well,
    Both the unseen and the seen;
Make the house, where Gods may dwell,
    Beautiful, entire, and clean.

Else our lives are incomplete,
    Standing in these walls of Time,
Broken stairways, where the feet
    Stumble as they seek to climb.

Build to-day, then, strong and sure,
    With a firm and ample base;
And ascending and secure
    Shall to-morrow find its place.

Thus alone can we attain
    To those turrets, where the eye
Sees the world as one vast plain,
    And one boundless reach of sky.

My Cathedral

Like two cathedral towers these stately pines
    Uplift their fretted summits tipped with
        cones;

The arch beneath them is not built with
   stones,
Not Art but Nature traced these lovely lines,
And carved this graceful arabesque of vines;
   No organ but the wind here sighs and moans,
   No sepulchre conceals a martyr's bones,
   No marble bishop on his tomb reclines.
Enter! the pavement, carpeted with leaves,
   Gives back a softened echo to thy tread!
   Listen! the choir is singing; all the birds,
In leafy galleries beneath the eaves,
   Are singing! listen, ere the sound be fled,
And learn there may be worship without words.

Poems by
John Greenleaf Whittier

My Playmate

The pines were dark on Ramoth hill,
    Their song was soft and low;
The blossoms in the sweet May wind
    Were falling like the snow.

The blossoms drifted at our feet,
    The orchard birds sang clear;
The sweetest and the saddest day
    It seemed of all the year.

For, more to me than birds or flowers,
    My playmate left her home,
And took with her the laughing spring,
    The music and the bloom.

She kissed the lips of kith and kin,
    She laid her hand in mine:
What more could ask the bashful boy
    Who fed her father's kine?

She left us in the bloom of May:
    The constant years told o'er
Their seasons with as sweet May morns,
    But she came back no more.

I walk, with noiseless feet, the round
    Of uneventful years;

Still o'er and o'er I sow the spring
  And reap the autumn ears.

She lives where all the golden year
  Her summer roses blow;
The dusky children of the sun
  Before her come and go.

There haply with her jewelled hands
  She smooths her silken gown,—
No more the homespun lap wherein
  I shook the walnuts down.

The wild grapes wait us by the brook,
  The brown nuts on the hill,
And still the May-day flowers make sweet
  The woods of Follymill.

The lilies blossom in the pond,
  The bird builds in the tree,
The dark pines sing on Ramoth hill
  The slow song of the sea.

I wonder if she thinks of them,
  And how the old time seems,—
If ever the pines of Ramoth wood
  Are sounding in her dreams.

I see her face, I hear her voice;
 Does she remember mine?
And what to her is now the boy
 Who fed her father's kine?

What cares she that the orioles build
 For other eyes than ours,—
That other hands with nuts are filled,
 And other laps with flowers?

O playmate in the golden time!
 Our mossy seat is green,
Its fringing violets blossom yet,
 The old trees o'er it lean.

The winds so sweet with birch and fern
 A sweeter memory blow;
And there is spring the veeries sing
 The song of long ago.

And still the pines of Ramoth wood
 Are moaning like the sea,—
The moaning of the sea of change
 Between myself and thee!

My Triumph

The autumn-time has come;
On woods that dream of bloom,
And over purpling vines,
The low sun fainter shines.

The aster-flower is failing,
The hazel's gold is paling;
Yet overhead more near
The eternal stars appear!

And present gratitude
Insures the future's good,
And for the things I see
I trust the things to be;

That in the paths untrod,
And the long days of God,
My feet shall still be led,
My heart be comforted.

O living friends who love me!
O dear ones gone above me!
Careless of other fame,
I leave to you my name.

Hide it from idle praises,
Save it from evil phrases:
Why, when dear lips that spake it
Are dumb, should strangers wake it?

Let the thick curtain fall;
I better know than all
How little I have gained,
How vast the unattained.

Not by the page word-painted
Let life be banned or sainted:
Deeper than written scroll
The colors of the soul.

Sweeter than any sung
My songs that found no tongue;
Nobler than any fact
My wish that failed of act.

Others shall sing the song,
Others shall right the wrong,—
Finish what I begin,
And all I fail of win.

What matter, I or they?
Mine or another's day,
So the right word be said
And life the sweeter made?

Hail to the coming singers!
Hail to the brave light-bringers!
Forward I reach and share
All that they sing and dare.

The airs of heaven blow o'er me;
A glory shines before me

Of what mankind shall be,—
Pure, generous, brave, and free.

A dream of man and woman
Diviner but still human,
Solving the riddle old,
Shaping the Age of Gold!

The love of God and neighbor;
An equal-handed labor;
The richer life, where beauty
Walks hand in hand with duty.

Ring, bells in unreared steeples,
The joy of unborn peoples!
Sound, trumpets far off blown,
Your triumph is my own!

Parcel and part of all,
I keep the festival,
Fore-reach the good to be,
And share the victory.

I feel the earth more sunward,
I join the great march onward,
And take, by faith, while living,
My freehold of thanksgiving.

What the Birds Said

The birds against the April wind
    Flew northward, singing as they flew;
They sang, "The land we leave behind
    Has swords for corn-blades, blood for dew."

"O wild-birds, flying from the South,
    What saw and heard ye, gazing down?"
"We saw the mortar's upturned mouth,
    The sickened camp, the blazing town!

"Beneath the bivouac's starry lamps,
    We saw your march-worn children die;
In shrouds of moss, in cypress swamps,
    We saw your dead uncoffined lie.

"We heard the starving prisoner's sighs,
    And saw, from line and trench, your sons
Follow our flight with home-sick eyes
    Beyond the battery's smoking guns."

"And heard and saw ye only wrong
    And pain," I cried, "O wing-worn flocks?"
"We heard," they sang, "the freedman's song,
    The crash of Slavery's broken locks!

"We saw from new, uprising States
    The treason-nursing mischief spurned,
As, crowding Freedom's ample gates,
    The long-estranged and lost returned.

"O'er dusky faces, seamed and old,
    And hands horn-hard with unpaid toil,
  With hope in every rustling fold,
    We saw your star-dropt flag uncoil.

"And struggling up through sounds accursed,
    A grateful murmur clomb the air;
  A whisper scarcely heard at first,
    It filled the listening heavens with prayer.

"And sweet and far, as from a star,
    Replied a voice which shall not cease,
  Till, drowning all the noise of war,
    It sings the blessed song of peace!"

So to me, in a doubtful day
    Of chill and slowly greening spring,
  Low stooping from the cloudy gray,
    The wild-birds sang or seemed to sing.

They vanished in the misty air,
    The song went with them in their flight;
  But lo! they left the sunset fair,
    And in the evening there was light.

The Eternal Goodness

O friends! with whom my feet have trod
  The quiet aisles of prayer,
Glad witness to your zeal for God
  And love of man I bear.

I trace your lines of argument;
  Your logic linked and strong
I weigh as one who dreads dissent,
  And fears a doubt as wrong.

But still my human hands are weak
  To hold your iron creeds:
Against the words ye bid me speak
  My heart within me pleads.

Who fathoms the Eternal Thought?
  Who talks of scheme and plan?
The Lord is God! He needeth not
  The poor device of man.

I walk with bare, hushed feet the ground
  Ye tread with boldness shod;
I dare not fix with mete and bound
  The love and power of God.

Ye praise His justice; even such
  His pitying love I deem:
Ye seek a king; I fain would touch
  The robe that hath no seam.

Ye see the curse which overbroods
  A world of pain and loss;
I hear our Lord's beatitudes
  And prayer upon the cross.

More than your schoolmen teach, within
  Myself, alas! I know:
Too dark ye cannot paint the sin,
  Too small the merit show.

I bow my forehead to the dust,
  I veil mine eyes for shame,
And urge, in trembling self-distrust,
  A prayer without a claim.

I see the wrong that round me lies,
  I feel the guilt within;
I hear, with groan and travail-cries,
  The world confess its sin.

Yet, in the maddening maze of things,
  And tossed by storm and flood,
To one fixed trust my spirit clings;
  I know that God is good!

Not mine to look where cherubim
  And seraphs may not see,
But nothing can be good in Him
  Which evil is in me.

The wrong that pains my soul below
  I dare not throne above,

I know not of His hate,—I know
　　His goodness and His love.

I dimly guess from blessings known
　　Of greater out of sight,
And, with the chastened Psalmist, own
　　His judgments too are right.

I long for household voices gone,
　　For vanished smiles I long,
But God hath led my dear ones on,
　　And He can do no wrong.

I know not what the future hath
　　Of marvel or surprise,
Assured alone that life and death
　　His mercy underlies.

And if my heart and flesh are weak
　　To bear an untried pain,
The bruisëd reed He will not break,
　　But strengthen and sustain.

No offering of my own I have,
　　Nor works my faith to prove;
I can but give the gifts He gave,
　　And plead His love for love.

And so beside the Silent Sea
   I wait the muffled oar;
No harm from Him can come to me
   On ocean or on shore.

I know not where His islands lift
   Their fronded palms in air;
I only know I cannot drift
   Beyond His love and care.

O brothers! if my faith is vain,
   If hopes like these betray,
Pray for me that my feet may gain
   The sure and safer way.

And Thou, O Lord! by whom are seen
   Thy creatures as they be,
Forgive me if too close I lean
   My human heart on Thee!

From "Snow-Bound"

A winter idyl

The sun that brief December day
Rose cheerless over hills of gray,
And, darkly circled, gave at noon
A sadder light than waning moon.
Slow tracing down the thickening sky
Its mute and ominous prophecy,
A portent seeming less than threat,

It sank from sight before it set.
A chill no coat, however stout,
Of homespun stuff could quite shut out,
A hard, dull bitterness of cold,
That checked, mid-vein, the circling race
Of life-blood in the sharpened face,
The coming of the snow-storm told.
The wind blew east; we heard the roar
Of Ocean on his wintry shore,
And felt the strong pulse throbbing there
Beat with low rhythm our inland air.

Meanwhile we did our nightly chores,—
Brought in the wood from out of doors,
Littered the stalls, and from the mows
Raked down the herd's-grass for the cows:
Heard the horse whinnying for his corn;
And, sharply clashing horn on horn,
Impatient down the stanchion rows
The cattle shake their walnut bows;
While, peering from his early perch
Upon the scaffold's pole of birch,
The cock his crested helmet bent
And down his querulous challenge sent.

Unwarmed by any sunset light
The gray day darkened into night,
A night made hoary with the swarm
And whirl-dance of the blinding storm,
As zigzag, wavering to and fro,
Crossed and recrossed the wingèd snow:
And ere the early bedtime came

The white drift piled the window-frame,
And through the glass the clothes-line posts
Looked in like tall and sheeted ghosts.

So all night long the storm roared on:
The morning broke without a sun;
In tiny spherule traced with lines
Of Nature's geometric signs,
In starry flake, and pellicle,
All day the hoary meteor fell;
And, when the second morning shone,
We looked upon a world unknown,
On nothing we could call our own.
Around the glistening wonder bent
The blue walls of the firmament,
No cloud above, no earth below,—
A universe of sky and snow!
The old familiar sights of ours
Took marvellous shapes; strange domes and
    towers
Rose up where sty or corn-crib stood,
Or garden-wall, or belt of wood;
A smooth white mound the brush-pile showed,
A fenceless drift what once was road;
The bridle-post an old man sat
With loose-flung coat and high cocked hat;
The well-curb had a Chinese roof;
And even the long sweep, high aloof,
In its slant splendor, seemed to tell
Of Pisa's leaning miracle.

A prompt, decisive man, no breath
Our father wasted: "Boys, a path!"
Well pleased, (for when did farmer boy
Count such a summons less than joy?)
Our buskins on our feet we drew;
With mittened hands, and caps drawn low,
To guard our necks and ears from snow,
We cut the solid whiteness through.
And, where the drift was deepest, made
A tunnel walled and overlaid
With dazzling crystal: we had read
Of rare Aladdin's wondrous cave,
And to our own his name we gave,
With many a wish the luck were ours
To test his lamp's supernal powers.
We reached the barn with merry din,
And roused the prisoned brutes within.
The old horse thrust his long head out,
And grave with wonder gazed about;
The cock his lusty greeting said,
And forth his speckled harem led;
The oxen lashed their tails, and hooked,
And mild reproach of hunger looked;
The hornëd patriarch of the sheep,
Like Egypt's Amun roused from sleep,
Shook his sage head with gesture mute,
And emphasized with stamp of foot.

All day the gusty north-wind bore
The loosening drift its breath before;
Low circling round its southern zone,
The sun through dazzling snow-mist shone.

No church-bell lent its Christian tone
To the savage air, no social smoke
Curled over woods of snow-hung oak.
A solitude made more intense
By dreary-voicëd elements,
The shrieking of the mindless wind,
The moaning tree-boughs swaying blind,
And on the glass the unmeaning beat
Of ghostly finger-tips of sleet.
Beyond the circle of our hearth
No welcome sound of toil or mirth
Unbound the spell, and testified
Of human life and thought outside.
We minded that the sharpest ear
The buried brooklet could not hear,
The music of whose liquid lip
Had been to us companionship,
And, in our lonely life, had grown
To have an almost human tone.

As night drew on, and, from the crest
Of wooded knolls that ridged the west,
The sun, a snow-blown traveller, sank
From sight beneath the smothering bank,
We piled, with care, our nightly stack
Of wood against the chimney-back,—
The oaken log, green, huge, and thick,
And on its top the stout back-stick;
The knotty forestick laid apart,
And filled between with curious art
The ragged brush; then, hovering near,
We watched the first red blaze appear,

Heard the sharp crackle, caught the gleam
On whitewashed wall and sagging beam,
Until the old, rude-furnished room
Burst, flower-like, into rosy bloom;
While radiant with a mimic flame
Outside the sparkling drift became,
And through the bare-boughted lilac-tree
Our own warm hearth seemed blazing free.
The crane and pendent trammels showed,
The Turks' heads on the andirons glowed;
While childish fancy, prompt to tell
The meaning of the miracle,
Whispered the old rhyme: *"Under the tree,*
When fire outdoors burns merrily,
There the witches are making tea."

Poems by
Edgar Allan Poe

To My Mother

Because I feel that, in the Heavens above,
    The angels, whispering to one another,
Can find, among their burning terms of love,
    None so devotional as that of "Mother,"
Therefore by that dear name I long have called
        you—
    You who are more than mother unto me,
And fill my heart of hearts, where Death
        installed you
    In setting my Virginia's spirit free.
My mother—my own mother, who died early,
    Was but the mother of myself; but you
Are mother to the one I loved so dearly,
    And thus are dearer than the mother I knew
By that infinity with which my wife
    Was dearer to my soul than its soul-life.

Sonnet—To Science

Science! true daughter of Old Time thou art!
    Who alterest all things with thy peering
        eyes.
Why preyest thou thus upon the poet's
        heart,
    Vulture, whose wings are dull realities?

181

How should he love thee? or how deem thee
　　wise?
　　Who wouldst not leave him in his
　　wandering
To seek for treasure in the jeweled skies,
　　Albeit he soared with an undaunted wing?
Hast thou not dragged Diana from her car?
　　And driven the Hamadryad from the
　　wood
To seek a shelter in some happier star?
　　Hast thou not torn the Naiad from her
　　flood,
The Elfin from the green grass, and from
　　me
The summer dream beneath the tamarind
　　tree?

Poems by
Alfred Lord Tennyson

The Oak

Live thy Life,
   Young and old,
Like yon oak,
Bright in spring,
   Living gold;

Summer-rich
   Then; and then
Autumn-changed,
Soberer-hued
   Gold again.

All his leaves
   Fall'n at length,
Look, he stands,
Trunk and bough,
   Naked strength.

The Lotos-Eaters

"Courage!" he said, and pointed toward the
   land,
"This mounting wave will roll us shoreward
   soon."
In the afternoon they came unto a land
In which it seeméd always afternoon.

All round the coast the languid air did swoon,
Breathing like one that hath a weary dream.
Full-faced above the valley stood the moon;
And, like a downward smoke, the slender
  stream
Along the cliff to fall and pause and fall did
  seem.

A land of streams! some, like a downward
  smoke,
Slow-dropping veils of thinnest lawn, did go;
And some through wavering lights and shadows
  broke,
Rolling a slumbrous sheet of foam below.
They saw the gleaming river seaward flow
From the inner land; far off, three
  mountaintops
Three silent pinnacles of aged snow,
Stood sunset-flushed; and, dewed with showery
  drops,
Up-clomb the shadowy pine above the woven
  copse.

The charméd sunset lingered low adown
In the red West; through mountain clefts the
  dale
Was seen far inland, and the yellow down
Bordered with palm, and many a winding vale
And meadow, set with slender galingale;
A land where all things always seemed the
  same!
And round about the keel with faces pale,

Dark faces pale against that rosy flame,
The mild-eyed melancholy Lotos-eaters came.

Branches they bore of that enchanted stem,
Laden with flower and fruit, whereof they gave
To each, but whoso did receive of them
And taste, to him the gushing of the wave
Far far away did seem to mourn and rave
On alien shores; and if his fellow spake,
His voice was thin, as voices from the grave;
And deep-asleep he seemed, yet all awake,
And music in his ears his beating heart did
    make.

They sat them down upon the yellow sand,
Between the sun and moon upon the shore;
And sweet it was to dream of Fatherland,
Of child, and wife, and slave; but evermore
Most weary seemed the sea, weary the oar,
Weary the wandering fields of barren foam.
Then some one said, "We will return no more";
And all at once they sang, "Our island home
Is far beyond the wave; we will no longer
    roam."

Choric Song

1

There is sweet music here that softer falls
Than petals from blown roses on the grass,
Or night-dews on still waters between walls
Of shadowy granite, in a gleaming pass;

187

Music that gentlier on the spirit lies,
Than tired eyelids upon tired eyes;
Music that brings sweet sleep down from the
  blissful skies.
Here are cool mosses deep,
And through the moss the ivies creep,
And in the stream the long-leaved flowers weep,
And from the craggy ledge the poppy hangs in
  sleep.

2

Why are we weighed upon with heaviness,
And utterly consumed with sharp distress,
While all things else have rest from weariness?
All things have rest: why should we toil alone,
We only toil, who are the first of things,
And make perpetual moan,
Still from one sorrow to another thrown;
Nor ever fold our wings,
And cease from wanderings,
Nor steep our brows in slumber's holy balm;
Nor harken what the inner spirit sings,
"There is no joy but calm!"—
Why should we only toil, the roof and crown of
  things?

3

Lo! in the middle of the wood,
The folded leaf is wooed from out the bud
With winds upon the branch, and there
Grows green and broad, and takes no care,
Sun-steeped at noon, and in the moon

188

Nightly dew-fed; and turning yellow
Falls, and floats adown the air.
Lo! sweetened with the summer light,
The full-juiced apple, waxing over-mellow,
Drops in a silent autumn night.
All its allotted length of days
The flower ripens in its place,
Ripens and fades, and falls, and hath no
    toil,
Fast-rooted in the fruitful soil.

4

Hateful is the dark blue sky,
Vaulted o'er the dark blue sea.
Death is the end of life; ah, why
Should life all labor be?
Let us alone. Time driveth onward fast,
And in a little while our lips are dumb.
Let us alone. What is it that will last?
All things are taken from us, and become
Portions and parcels of the dreadful past.
Let us alone. What pleasure can we have
To war with evil? Is there any peace
In ever climbing up the climbing wave?
All things have rest, and ripen toward the
    grave
In silence—ripen, fall, and cease:
Give us long rest or death, dark death, or
    dreamful ease.

How sweet it were, hearing the downward
  stream,
With half-shut eyes ever to seem
Falling asleep in a half-dream!
To dream and dream, like yonder amber light,
Which will not leave the myrrh-bush on the
  height;
To hear each other's whispered speech;
Eating the Lotos day by day,
To watch the crisping ripples on the beach,
And tender curving lines of creamy spray;
To lend our hearts and spirits wholly
To the influence of mild-minded melancholy;
To muse and brood and live again in memory,
With those old faces of our infancy
Heaped over with a mound of grass,
Two handfuls of white dust, shut in an urn of
  brass!

Dear is the memory of our wedded lives,
And dear the last embraces of our wives
And their warm tears; but all hath suffered
  change;
For surely now our household hearths are cold,
Our sons inherit us, our looks are strange,
And we should come like ghosts to trouble joy.
Or else the island princes overbold
Have eat our substance, and the minstrel sings
Before them of the ten years' war in Troy,
And our great deeds, as half-forgotten things.

Is there confusion in the little isle?
Let what is broken so remain.
The Gods are hard to reconcile;
'Tis hard to settle order once again.
There *is* confusion worse than death,
Trouble on trouble, pain on pain,
Long labor unto aged breath,
Sore tasks to hearts worn out by many wars
And eyes grown dim with gazing on the pilot-
    stars.

7

But, propped on beds of amaranth and moly,
How sweet—while warm airs lull us, blowing
    lowly—
With half-dropped eyelid still,
Beneath a heaven dark and holy,
To watch the long bright river drawing slowly
His waters from the purple hill—
To hear the dewy echoes calling
From cave to cave through the thick-twined vine—
To watch the emerald-colored water falling
Through many a woven acanthus wreath divine!
Only to hear and see the far-off sparkling brine,
Only to hear were sweet, stretched out beneath
    the pine.

8

The Lotos blooms below the barren peak,
The Lotos blows by every winding creek;
All day the wind breathes low with mellower
    tone;

Through every hollow cave and alley lone
Round and round the spicy downs the yellow
　　Lotos dust is blown.
We have had enough of action, and of motion
　　we,
Rolled to starboard, rolled to larboard, when
　　the surge was seething free,
Where the wallowing monster spouted his foam-
　　fountains in the sea.
Let us swear an oath, and keep it with an equal
　　mind,
In the hollow Lotos land to live and lie reclined
On the hills like Gods together, careless of
　　mankind.
For they lie beside their nectar, and the bolts
　　are hurled
Far below them in the valleys, and the clouds
　　are lightly curled
Round their golden houses, girdled with the
　　gleaming world;
Where they smile in secret, looking over wasted
　　lands,
Blight and famine, plague and earthquake,
　　roaring deeps and fiery sands,
Clanging fights, and flaming towns, and sinking
　　ships, and praying hands.
But they smile, they find a music centered in a
　　doleful song
Steaming up, a lamentation and an ancient tale
　　of wrong,
Like a tale of little meaning though the words
　　are strong;

Chanted from an ill-used race of men that cleave
   the soil,
Sow the seed, and reap the harvest with
   enduring toil,
Storing yearly little dues of wheat, and wine and
   oil;
Till they perish and they suffer—some, 'tis
   whispered—down in hell
Suffer endless anguish, others in Elysian valleys
   dwell,
Resting weary limbs at last on beds of asphodel.
Surely, surely, slumber is more sweet than toil,
   the shore
Than labor in the deep mid-ocean, wind and
   wave and oar;
O, rest ye, brother mariners, we will not
   wander more.

A Farewell

Flow down, cold rivulet, to the sea,
   Thy tribute wave deliver:
No more by thee my steps shall be,
   For ever and for ever.

Flow, softly flow, by lawn and lea,
   A rivulet then a river:
No where by thee my steps shall be,
   For ever and for ever.

But here will sigh thine alder tree,
    And here thine aspen shiver;
And here by thee will hum the bee,
    For ever and for ever.

A thousand suns will stream on thee,
    A thousand moons will quiver;
But not by thee my steps shall be,
    For ever and for ever.

The Grandmother

I

And Willy, my eldest-born, is gone, you say,
    little Anne?
Ruddy and white, and strong on his legs, he
    looks like a man.
And Willy's wife has written: she never was
    over-wise,
Never the wife for Willy: he wouldn't take my
    advice.

II

For, Annie, you see, her father was not the man
    to save,
Hadn't a head to manage, and drank himself
    into his grave.
Pretty enough, very pretty! but I was against it
    for one.
Eh!—but he wouldn't hear me—and Willy, you
    say, is gone.

194

III

Willy, my beauty, my eldest-born, the flower of
    the flock;
Never a man could fling him: for Willy stood
    like a rock.
'Here's a leg for a babe of a week!' says doctor;
    and he would be bound,
There was not his like that year in twenty
    parishes round.

IV

Strong of his hands, and strong on his legs, but
    still of his tongue!
I ought to have gone before him: I wonder he
    went so young.
I cannot cry for him, Annie: I have not long to
    stay;
Perhaps I shall see him the sooner, for he lived
    far away.

V

Why do you look at me, Annie? you think I am
    hard and cold;
But all my children have gone before me, I am
    so old:
I cannot weep for Willy, nor can I weep for the
    rest;
Only at your age, Annie, I could have wept
    with the best.

VI

For I remember a quarrel I had with your
    father, my dear,
All for a slanderous story, that cost me many a
    tear.
I mean your grandfather, Annie: it cost me a
    world of woe,
Seventy years ago, my darling, seventy years
    ago.

VII

For Jenny, my cousin, had come to the place,
    and I knew right well
That Jenny had tript in her time: I knew, but I
    would not tell.
And she to be coming and slandering me, the
    base little liar!
But the tongue is a fire as you know, my dear,
    the tongue is a fire.

VIII

And the parson made it his text that week, and
    he said likewise,
That a lie which is half a truth is ever the
    blackest of lies,
That a lie which is all a lie may be met and
    fought with outright,
But a lie which is part a truth is a harder matter
    to fight.

IX

And Willy had not been down to the farm for a
　week and a day;
And all things look'd half-dead, tho' it was the
　middle of May.
Jenny, to slander me, who knew what Jenny
　had been!
But soiling another, Annie, will never make
　oneself clean.

X

And I cried myself well-nigh blind, and all of an
　evening late
I climb'd to the top of the garth, and stood by
　the road at the gate.
The moon like a rick on fire was rising over the
　dale,
And whit, whit, whit, in the bush beside me
　chirrupt the nightingale.

XI

All of a sudden he stopt: there past by the gate
　of the farm,
Willy,—he didn't see me,—and Jenny hung on
　his arm.
Out into the road I started, and spoke I scarce
　knew how;
Ah, there's no fool like the old one—it makes
　me angry now.

Willy stood up like a man, and look'd the thing
  that he meant;
Jenny, the viper, made me a mocking curtsey
  and went.
And I said, 'Let us part: in a hundred years it'll
  all be the same,
You cannot love me at all, if you love not my
  good name.'

And he turn'd, and I saw his eyes all wet, in the
  sweet moonshine:
'Sweetheart, I love you so well that your good
  name is mine.
And what do I care for Jane, let her speak of
  you well or ill;
But marry me out of hand: we two shall be
  happy still.'

'Marry you, Willy!' said I, 'but I needs must
  speak my mind,
And I fear you'll listen to tales, be jealous and
  hard and unkind.'
But he turn'd and claspt me in his arms, and
  answer'd, 'No, love, no;'
Seventy years ago, my darling, seventy years
  ago.

XV

So Willy and I were wedded: I wore a lilac
  gown;
And the ringers rang with a will, and he gave
  the ringers a crown.
But the first that ever I bare was dead before he
  was born,
Shadow and shine is life, little Annie, flower
  and thorn.

XVI

That was the first time, too, that ever I thought
  of death.
There lay the sweet little body that never had
  drawn a breath.
I had not wept, little Anne, not since I had
  been a wife;
But I wept like a child that day, for the babe
  had fought for his life.

XVII

His dear little face was troubled, as if with
  anger or pain:
I look'd at the still little body—his trouble had
  all been in vain.
For Willy I cannot weep, I shall see him
  another morn:
But I wept like a child for the child that was
  dead before he was born.

XVIII

But he cheer'd me, my good man, for he
  seldom said me nay:
Kind, like a man, was he; like a man, too,
  would have his way:
Never jealous—not he: we had many a happy
  year;
And he died, and I could not weep—my own
  time seem'd so near.

XIX

But I wish'd it had been God's will that I, too,
  then could have died:
I began to be tired a little, and fain had slept at
  his side.
And that was ten years back, or more, if I don't
  forget:
But as to the children, Annie, they're all about
  me yet.

XX

Pattering over the boards, my Annie who left
  me at two,
Patter she goes, my own little Annie, an Annie
  like you:
Pattering over the boards, she comes and goes
  at her will,
While Harry is in the five-acre and Charlie
  ploughing the hill.

XXI

And Harry and Charlie, I hear them too—they
    sing to their team:
Often they come to the door in a pleasant kind
    of a dream.
They come and sit by my chair, they hover
    about my bed—
I am not always certain if they be alive or dead.

XXII

And yet I know for a truth, there's none of
    them left alive;
For Harry went at sixty, your father at sixty-
    five:
And Willy, my eldest-born, at nigh threescore
    and ten;
I knew them all as babies, and now they're
    elderly men.

XXIII

For mine is a time of peace, it is not often I
    grieve;
I am oftener sitting at home in my father's farm
    at eve:
And the neighbours come and laugh and gossip,
    and so do I;
I find myself often laughing at things that have
    long gone by.

XXIV

To be sure the preacher says, our sins should
make us sad:
But mine is a time of peace, and there is Grace
to be had;
And God, not man, is the Judge of us all when
life shall cease;
And in this Book, little Annie, the message is
one of Peace.

XXV

And age is a time of peace, so it be free from
pain,
And happy has been my life; but I would not
live it again.
I seem to be tired a little, that's all, and long for
rest;
Only at your age, Annie, I could have wept
with the best.

XXVI

So Willy has gone, my beauty, my eldest-born,
my flower;
But how can I weep for Willy, he has but gone
for an hour,—
Gone for a minute, my son, from this room into
the next;
I, too, shall go in a minute. What time have I to
be vext?

XXVII

And Willy's wife has written, she never was
over-wise.
Get me my glasses, Annie: thank God that I
keep my eyes.
There is but a trifle left you, when I shall have
past away.
But stay with the old woman now: you cannot
have long to stay.

The May Queen

You must wake and call me early, call me early,
mother dear;
To-morrow 'ill be the happiest time of all the
glad New-year;
Of all the glad New-year, mother, the maddest
merriest day;
For I'm to be Queen o' the May, mother, I'm
to be Queen o' the May.

There's many a black black eye, they say, but
none so bright as mine;
There's Margaret and Mary, there's Kate and
Caroline:
But none so fair as little Alice in all the land
they say,
So I'm to be Queen o' the May, mother, I'm to
be Queen o' the May.

203

I sleep so sound all night, mother, that I shall never wake,
If you do not call me loud when the day begins to break:
But I must gather knots of flowers, and buds and garlands gay,
For I'm to be Queen o' the May, mother, I'm to be Queen o' the May.

As I came up the valley whom think ye should I see,
But Robin leaning on the bridge beneath the hazel-tree?
He thought of that sharp look, mother, I gave him yesterday,
But I'm to be Queen o' the May, mother, I'm to be Queen o' the May.

He thought I was a ghost, mother, for I was all in white,
And I ran by him without speaking, like a flash of light.
They call me cruel-hearted, but I care not what they say,
For I'm to be Queen o' the May, mother, I'm to be Queen o' the May.

They say he's dying all for love, but that can never be:
They say his heart is breaking, mother—what is that to me?

There's many a bolder lad 'ill woo me any
  summer day,
And I'm to be Queen o' the May, mother, I'm
  to be Queen o' the May.

Little Effie shall go with me to-morrow to the
  green,
And you'll be there, too, mother, to see me
  made the Queen;
For the shepherd lads on every side 'ill come
  from far away,
And I'm to be Queen o' the May, mother, I'm
  to be Queen o' the May.

The honeysuckle round the porch has wov'n its
  wavy bowers,
And by the meadow-trenches blow the faint
  sweet cuckoo-flowers;
And the wild marsh-marigold shines like fire in
  swamps and hollows gray,
And I'm to be Queen o' the May, mother, I'm
  to be Queen o' the May.

The night-winds come and go, mother, upon
  the meadow-grass,
And the happy stars above them seem to
  brighten as they pass;
There will not be a drop of rain the whole of
  the livelong day,
And I'm to be Queen o' the May, mother, I'm
  to be Queen o' the May.

All the valley, mother, 'ill be fresh and green
 and still,
And the cowslip and the crowfoot are over all
 the hill,
And the rivulet in the flowery dale 'ill merrily
 glance and play,
For I'm to be Queen o' the May, mother, I'm
 to be Queen o' the May.

So you must wake and call me early, call me
 early, mother dear,
To-morrow 'ill be the happiest time of all the
 glad New-year:
To-morrow 'ill be of all the year the maddest
 merriest day,
For I'm to be Queen o' the May, mother, I'm
 to be Queen o' the May.

NEW-YEAR'S EVE

If you're waking call me early, call me early,
 mother dear,
For I would see the sun rise upon the glad
 New-year.
It is the last New-year that I shall ever see,
Then you may lay me low i' the mould and
 think no more of me.

To-night I saw the sun set: he set and left
 behind
The good old year, the dear old time, and all
 my peace of mind;

206

And the New-year's coming up, mother, but I
    shall never see
The blossom on the blackthorn, the leaf upon
    the tree.

Last May we made a crown of flowers: we had
    a merry day;
Beneath the hawthorn on the green they made
    me Queen of May;
And we danced about the may-pole and in the
    hazel copse,
Till Charles's Wain came out above the tall
    white chimney-tops.

There's not a flower on all the hills: the frost is
    on the pane:
I only wish to live till the snowdrops come
    again:
I wish the snow would melt and the sun come
    out on high:
I long to see a flower so before the day I die.

The building rook 'ill caw from the windy tall
    elm-tree,
And the tufted plover pipe along the fallow lea,
And the swallow 'ill come back again with
    summer o'er the wave,
But I shall lie alone, mother, within the
    mouldering grave.

Upon the chancel-casement, and upon that
    grave of mine,
In the early early morning the summer sun 'ill
    shine,
Before the red cock crows from the farm upon
    the hill,
When you are warm-asleep, mother, and all the
    world is still.

When the flowers come again, mother, beneath
    the waning light
You'll never see me more in the long gray fields
    at night;
When from the dry dark wold the summer airs
    blow cool
On the oat-grass and the sword-grass, and the
    bulrush in the pool.

You'll bury me, my mother, just beneath the
    hawthorn shade,
And you'll come sometimes and see me where I
    am lowly laid.
I shall not forget you, mother, I shall hear you
    when you pass,
With your feet above my head in the long and
    pleasant grass.

I have been wild and wayward, but you'll
    forgive me now;
You'll kiss me, my own mother, and forgive me
    ere I go;

Nay, nay, you must not weep, nor let your
  grief be wild,
You should not fret for me, mother, you have
  another child.

If I can I'll come again, mother, from out my
  resting-place;
Tho' you'll not see me, mother, I shall look
  upon your face;
Tho' I cannot speak a word, I shall harken
  what you say,
And be often, often with you when you think
  I'm far away.

Goodnight, goodnight, when I have said
  goodnight for evermore,
And you see me carried out from the threshold
  of the door;
Don't let Effie come to see me till my grave be
  growing green:
She'll be a better child to you than ever I have
  been.

She'll find my garden-tools upon the granary
  floor:
Let her take 'em: they are hers: I shall never
  garden more:
But tell her, when I'm gone, to train the
  rosebush that I set
About the parlour-window and the box of
  mignonette.

Goodnight, sweet mother: call me before the
    day is born.
All night I lie awake, but I fall asleep at morn;
But I would see the sun rise upon the glad
    New-year,
So, if you're waking, call me, call me early,
    mother dear.

CONCLUSION

I thought to pass away before, and yet alive I
    am;
And in the fields all round I hear the bleating
    of the lamb.
How sadly, I remember, rose the morning of
    the year!
To die before the snowdrop came, and now the
    violet's here.

O sweet is the new violet, that comes beneath
    the skies,
And sweeter is the young lamb's voice to me
    that cannot rise,
And sweet is all the land about, and all the
    flowers that blow,
And sweeter far is death than life to me that
    long to go.

It seem'd so hard at first, mother, to leave the
    blessed sun,
And now it seems as hard to stay, and yet His
    will be done!

But still I think it can't be long before I find
    release;
And that good man, the clergyman, has told me
    words of peace.

O blessings on his kindly voice and on his silver
    hair!
And blessings on his whole life long, until he
    meet me there!
O blessings on his kindly heart and on his silver
    head!
A thousand times I blest him, as he knelt
    beside my bed.

He taught me all the mercy, for he show'd me
    all the sin.
Now, tho' my lamp was lighted late, there's
    One will let me in:
Nor would I now be well, mother, again if that
    could be,
For my desire is but to pass to Him that died
    for me.

I did not hear the dog howl, mother, or the
    death-watch beat,
There came a sweeter token when the night and
    morning meet:
But sit beside my bed, mother, and put your
    hand in mine,
And Effie on the other side, and I will tell the
    sign.

All in the wild March-morning I heard the
    angels call;
It was when the moon was setting, and the dark
    was over all;
The trees began to whisper, and the wind
    began to roll,
And in the wild March-morning I heard them
    call my soul.

For lying broad awake I thought of you and
    Effie dear;
I saw you sitting in the house, and I no longer
    here;
With all my strength I pray'd for both, and so I
    felt resign'd,
And up the valley came a swell of music on the
    wind.

I thought that it was fancy, and I listen'd in my
    bed,
And then did something speak to me—I know
    not what was said;
For great delight and shuddering took hold of
    all my mind,
And up the valley came again the music on the
    wind.

But you were sleeping; and I said, 'It's not for
    them: it's mine.'
And if it come three times, I thought, I take it
    for a sign.

And once again it came, and close beside the
 window-bars,
Then seem'd to go right up to Heaven and die
 among the stars.

So now I think my time is near. I trust it is. I
 know
The blessed music went that way my soul will
 have to go.
And for myself, indeed, I care not if I go to-
 day.
But, Effie, you must comfort *her* when I am
 past away.

And say to Robin a kind word, and tell him not
 to fret;
There's many a worthier than I, would make
 him happy yet.
If I had lived—I cannot tell—I might have
 been his wife;
But all these things have ceased to be, with my
 desire of life.

O look! the sun begins to rise, the heavens are
 in a glow;
He shines upon a hundred fields, and all of
 them I know.
And there I move no longer now, and there his
 light may shine—
Wild flowers in the valley for other hands than
 mine.

O sweet and strange it seems to me, that ere
  this day is done
The voice, that now is speaking, may be
  beyond the sun—
For ever and for ever with those just souls and
  true—
And what is life, that we should moan? why
  make we such ado?

For ever and for ever, all in a blessed home—
And there to wait a little while till you and
  Effie come—
To lie within the light of God, as I lie upon
  your breast—
And the wicked cease from troubling, and the
  weary are at rest.

Poems by
Robert Browning

Summum Bonum

All the breath and the bloom of the year in the
      bag of one bee:
All the wonder and wealth of the mine in the
      heart of one gem:
In the core of one pearl all the shade and the
      shine of the sea:
Breath and bloom, shade and shine,—
      wonder, wealth, and—how far above
      them
      Truth, that's brighter than gem,
      Trust, that's purer than pearl,—
Brightest truth, purest trust in the universe all
      were for me
      In the kiss of one girl.

Parting at Morning

Round the cape of a sudden came the sea,
And the sun looked over the mountain's rim:
And straight was a path of gold for him,
And the need of a world of men for me.

217

Two in the Campagna

1

I wonder do you feel today
  As I have felt since, hand in hand,
We sat down on the grass, to stray
  In spirit better through the land,
This morn of Rome and May?

2

For me, I touched a thought, I know,
  Has tantalized me many times,
(Like turns of thread the spiders throw
  Mocking across our path) for rhymes
To catch at and let go.

3

Help me to hold it! First it left
  The yellowing fennel, run to seed
There, branching from the brickwork's cleft,
  Some old tomb's ruin: yonder weed
Took up the floating weft,

4

Where one small orange cup amassed
  Five beetles—blind and green they grope
Among the honey-meal: and last,
  Everywhere on the grassy slope
I traced it. Hold it fast!

5

The champaign with its endless fleece
  Of feathery grasses everywhere!
Silence and passion, joy and peace,
  An everlasting wash of air—
Rome's ghost since her decease.

6

Such life here, through such lengths of hours,
  Such miracles performed in play,
Such primal naked forms of flowers,
  Such letting nature have her way
While heaven looks from its towers!

7

How say you? Let us, O my dove,
  Let us be unashamed of soul,
As earth lies bare to heaven above!
  How is it under our control
To love or not to love?

8

I would that you were all to me,
  You that are just so much, no more.
Nor yours nor mine, nor slave nor free!
  Where does the fault lie? What the core
O' the wound, since wound must be?

9

I would I could adopt your will,
  See with your eyes, and set my heart
Beating by yours, and drink my fill

At your soul's springs—your part my part
In life, for good and ill.

10

No. I yearn upward, touch you close,
  Then stand away. I kiss your cheek,
Catch your soul's warmth—I pluck the rose
  And love it more than tongue can speak—
Then the good minute goes.

11

Already how am I so far
  Out of that minute? Must I go
Still like the thistle-ball, no bar,
  Onward, whenever light winds blow,
Fixed by no friendly star?

12

Just when I seemed about to learn!
  Where is the thread now? Off again!
The old trick! Only I discern—
  Infinite passion, and the pain
Of finite hearts that yearn.

Epilogue to Asolando

At the midnight in the silence of the sleep-time,
  When you set your fancies free,
Will they pass to where—by death, fools think,
  imprisoned—

Low he lies who once so loved you, whom you
    loved so,
                —Pity me?

Oh to love so, be so loved, yet so mistaken!
    What had I on earth to do
With the slothful, with the mawkish, the
    unmanly?
Like the aimless, helpless, hopeless, did I drivel
                —Being—who?

One who never turned his back but marched
            breast forward,
    Never doubted clouds would break,
Never dreamed, though right were worsted,
    wrong would triumph,
Held we fall to rise, are baffled to fight better,
            Sleep to wake.

No, at noonday in the bustle of man's work-
    time
    Greet the unseen with a cheer!
Bid him forward, breast and back as either
    should be,
"Strive and thrive!" cry "Speed,—fight on, fare
    ever
            There as here!"

The Lost Leader

Just for a handful of silver he left us,
   Just for a riband to stick in his coat—
Found the one gift of which fortune bereft us,
   Lost all the others she lets us devote;
They, with the gold to give, doled him out
     silver,
   So much was theirs who so little allowed:
How all our copper had gone for his service!
   Rags—were they purple, his heart had been
     proud!
We that had loved him so, followed him,
     honored him,
   Lived in his mild and magnificent eye,
Learned his great language, caught his clear
     accents,
   Made him our pattern to live and to die!
Shakespeare was of us, Milton was for us,
   Burns, Shelley, were with us,—they watch
     from their graves!
He alone breaks from the van and the freemen,
   —He alone sinks to the rear and the slaves!

We shall march prospering,—not through his
     presence;
   Songs may inspirit us,—not from his lyre;
Deeds will be done,—while he boasts his
     quiescence,
   Still bidding crouch whom the rest bade
     aspire:

Blot out his name, then, record one lost soul
    more,
  One task more declined, one more footpath
      untrod,
One more devils'-triumph and sorrow for
    angels,
  One wrong more to man, one more insult to
      God!
Life's night begins: let him never come back to
    us!
  There would be doubt, hesitation and pain,
Forced praise on our part—the glimmer of
    twilight,
  Never glad confident morning again!
Best fight on well, for we taught him—strike
    gallantly,
  Menance our heart ere we master his own;
Then let him receive the new knowledge and
    wait us,
  Pardoned in heaven, the first by the throne!

Poems by
Edward Lear

There Was an Old Man with a Beard

There was an Old Man with a beard,
Who said, "It is just as I feared!—
Two Owls and a Hen, four Larks and a Wren,
Have all built their nests in my beard!"

Limerick

There was a young man in Iowa
Who exclaimed, "Where on earth shall I stow
          her!"
Of his sister he spoke, who was felled by an Oak
        Which abound in the plains of Iowa.

How Pleasant to Know Mr. Lear

How pleasant to know Mr. Lear!
   Who has written such volumes of stuff!
Some think him ill-tempered and queer,
   But a few think him pleasant enough.

His mind is concrete and fastidious,
   His nose is remarkably big;
His visage is more or less hideous,
   His beard it resembles a wig.

He has ears, and two eyes, and ten fingers,
    Leastways if you reckon two thumbs;
Long ago he was one of the singers,
    But now he is one of the dumbs.

He sits in a beautiful parlor,
    With hundreds of books on the wall;
He drinks a great deal of Marsala,
    But never gets tipsy at all.

He has many friends, laymen and clerical;
    Old Foss is the name of his cat;
His body is perfectly spherical,
    He weareth a runcible hat.

When he walks in a waterproof white,
    The children run after him so!
Calling out, "He's come out in his night-
    Gown, that crazy old Englishman, oh!"

He weeps by the side of the ocean,
    He weeps on the top of the hill;
He purchases pancakes and lotion,
    And chocolate shrimps from the mill.

He reads but he cannot speak Spanish,
    He cannot abide ginger-beer:
Ere the days of his pilgrimage vanish,
    How pleasant to know Mr. Lear!

Poems by
Henry David Thoreau

Great God, I Ask Thee
for No Meaner Pelf

Great God, I ask thee for no meaner pelf
Than that I may not disappoint myself,
That in my action I may soar as high,
As I can now discern with this clear eye.

And next in value, which thy kindness lends,
That I may greatly disappoint my friends,
Howe'er they think or hope that it may be,
They may not dream how thou'st distinguished
   me.

That my weak hand may equal my firm faith,
And my life practice more than my tongue
   saith;
That my low conduct may not show,
Nor my relenting lines,
That I thy purpose did not know,
Or overrated thy designs.

Haze

Woof of the sun, ethereal gauze,
Woven of Nature's richest stuffs,
Visible heat, air-water and dry sea,
Last conquest of the eye;

231

Toil of the day displayed, sun-dust,
Aerial surf upon the shores of earth,
Ethereal estuary, frith of light,
Breakers of air, billows of heat,
Fine summer spray on inland seas;
Bird of the sun, transparent-winged
Owlet of noon, soft-pinioned,
From heath or stubble rising without song,
Establish thy serenity o'er the fields.

I Am a Parcel of Vain Strivings Tied

I am a parcel of vain strivings tied
    By a chance bond together,
  Dangling this way and that, their links
    Were made so loose and wide,
            Methinks,
      For milder weather.

A bunch of violets without their roots,
    And sorrel intermixed,
  Encircled by a wisp of straw
    Once coiled about their shoots,
          The law
      By which I'm fixed.

A nosegay which Time clutched from out
   Those fair Elysian fields,
  With weeds and broken stems, in haste,
    Doth make the rabble rout
      That waste
   The day he yields.

And here I bloom for a short hour unseen,
   Drinking my juices up,
  With no root in the land
    To keep my branches green,
      But stand
   In a bare cup.

Within the Circuit of this Plodding Life

Within the circuit of this plodding life
There enter moments of an azure hue,
Untarnished fair as is the violet
Or anemone, when the spring strews them
By some meandering rivulet, which make
The best philosophy untrue that aims
But to console man for his grievances.
I have remembered when the winter came,
High in my chamber in the frosty nights,
When in the still light of the cheerful moon,
On every twig and rail and jutting spout,
The icy spears were adding to their length
Against the arrows of the coming sun,
How in the shimmering noon of summer past
Some unrecorded beam slanted across

The upland pastures where the Johnswort grew;
Or heard, amid the verdure of my mind,
The bee's long smothered hum, on the blue flag
Loitering amidst the mead; or busy rill,
Which now through all its course stands still
   and dumb
Its own memorial,—purling at its play
Along the slopes, and through the meadows
   next,
Until its youthful sound was hushed at last
In the staid current of the lowland stream;
Or seen the furrows shine but late upturned,
And where the fieldfare followed in the rear,
When all the fields around lay bound and hoar
Beneath a thick integument of snow.
So by God's cheap economy made rich
To go upon my winter's task again.

Poems by
Emily Brontë

Riches I Hold in Light Esteem

Riches I hold in light esteem
And Love I laugh to scorn
And lust of Fame was but a dream
That vanished with the morn—

And if I pray, the only prayer
That moves my lips for me
Is—"Leave the heart that now I bear
And give me liberty."

Yes, as my swift days near their goal
'Tis all that I implore—
Through life and death, a chainless soul
With courage to endure!

Stanzas

Often rebuked, yet always back returning
   To those first feelings that were born with
     me,
And leaving busy chase of wealth and learning
   For idle dreams of things which cannot be:

To-day, I will seek not the shadowy region;
   Its unsustaining vastness waxes drear;

And visions rising, legion after legion,
  Bring the unreal world too strangely near.

I'll walk, but not in old heroic traces,
  And not in paths of high morality,
And not among the half-distinguished faces,
  The clouded forms of long-past history.

I'll walk where my own nature would be
    leading:
  It vexes me to choose another guide:
Where the gray flocks in ferny glens are
    feeding;
  Where the wild wind blows on the mountain
    side.

What have those lonely mountains worth
    revealing?
  More glory and more grief than I can tell:
The earth that wakes *one* human heart to feeling
  Can centre both the worlds of Heaven and
    Hell.

Long Neglect Has Worn Away

Long neglect has worn away
Half the sweet enchanting smile;
Time has turned the bloom to gray;
Mold and damp the face defile.

238

But that lock of silky hair,
Still beneath the picture twined,
Tells what once those features were,
Paints their image on the mind.

Fair the hand that traced that line,
"Dearest, ever deem me true";
Swiftly flew the fingers fine
When the pen that motto drew.

Poems by
Walt Whitman

Joy, Shipmate, Joy!

Joy, shipmate, joy!
(Pleas'd to my soul at death I cry,)
Our life is closed, our life begins,
The long, long anchorage we leave,
The ship is clear at last, she leaps!
She swiftly courses from the shore,
Joy, shipmate, joy!

Miracles

Why, who makes much of a miracle?
As to me I know of nothing else but miracles,
Whether I walk the streets of Manhattan,
Or dart my sight over the roofs of houses
    toward the sky,
Or wade with naked feet along the beach just in
    the edge of the water,
Or stand under trees in the woods,
Or talk by day with any one I love, or sleep in
    the bed at night with any one I love,
Or sit at table at dinner with the rest,
Or look at strangers opposite me riding in the
    car,
Or watch honey-bees busy around the hive of a
    summer forenoon,
Or animals feeding in the fields,

Or birds, or the wonderfulness of insects in the
    air,
Or the wonderfulness of the sundown, or of
    stars shining so quiet and bright,
Or the exquisite delicate thin curve of the new
    moon in spring;
These with the rest, one and all, are to me
    miracles,
The whole referring, yet each distinct and in its
    place.

To me every hour of the light and dark is a
    miracle,
Every cubic inch of space is a miracle,
Every square yard of the surface of the earth is
    spread with the same,
Every foot of the interior swarms with the same.

To me the sea is a continual miracle,
The fishes that swim—the rocks—the motion of
    the waves—the ships with men in them,
What stranger miracles are there?

From "Song of Myself"

I think I could turn and live with animals,
    they're so placid and self-contain'd,
I stand and look at them long and long.

They do not sweat and whine about their
    condition,

They do not lie awake in the dark and weep for
  their sins,
They do not make me sick discussing their duty
  to God,
Not one is dissatisfied, not one is demented
  with the mania of owning things,
Not one kneels to another, nor to his kind that
  lived thousand of years ago,
Not one is respectable or unhappy over the
  whole earth.

Out of the Cradle Endlessly Rocking

Out of the cradle endlessly rocking,
Out of the mocking-bird's throat, the musical
  shuttle,
Out of the Ninth-month midnight,
Over the sterile sands and the fields beyond,
    where the child leaving his bed wander'd
        alone, bareheaded, barefoot,
Down from the shower'd halo,
Up from the mystic play of shadows twining
  and twisting as if they were alive,
Out from the patches of briers and blackberries,
From the memories of the bird that chanted to
  me,
From your memories sad brother, from the
  fitful risings and fallings I heard,
From under that yellow half-moon late-risen
  and swollen as if with tears,

245

From those beginning notes of yearning and
   love there in the mist,
From the thousand responses of my heart never
   to cease,
From the myraid thence-arous'd words,
From the word stronger and more delicious
   than any,
From such as now they start the scene
   revisiting,
As a flock, twittering, rising, or overhead
   passing,
Borne hither, ere all eludes me, hurriedly,
A man, yet by these tears a little boy again,
Throwing myself on the sand, confronting the
   waves,
I, chanter of pains and joys, uniter of here and
   hereafter,
Taking all hints to use them, but swiftly leaping
   beyond them,
A reminiscence sing.

Once Paumanok,
When the lilac-scent was in the air and Fifth-
   month grass was growing,
Up this seashore in some briers,
Two feather'd guests from Alabama, two
   together,
And their nest, and four light-green eggs
   spotted with brown,
And every day the he-bird to and fro near at
   hand,

And every day the she-bird crouch'd on her
    nest, silent, with bright eyes,
And every day I, a curious boy, never too close,
    never disturbing them,
Cautiously peering, absorbing, translating.

Shine! shine! shine!
Pour down your warmth, great sun!
While we bask, we two together.

Two together!
Winds blow south, or winds blow north,
Day come white, or night come black,
Home, or rivers and mountains from home,
Singing all time, minding no time,
While we two keep together.

Till of a sudden,
May-be kill'd, unknown to her mate,
One forenoon the she-bird crouch'd not on the
    nest,
Nor return'd that afternoon, nor the next,
Nor ever appear'd again.

And thenceforward all summer in the sound of
    the sea,
And at night under the full of the moon in
    calmer weather,
Over the hoarse surging of the sea,
Or flitting from brier to brier by day,

I saw, I heard at intervals the remaining one, the he-bird,
The solitary guest from Alabama.

Blow! blow! blow!
Blow up sea-winds along Paumanok's shore;
I wait and I wait till you blow my mate to me.

Yes, when the stars glisten'd,
All night long on the prong of a moss-scallop'd stake,
Down almost amid the slapping waves,
Sat the lone singer wonderful causing tears.

He call'd on his mate,
He pour'd forth the meanings which I of all men know.

Yes my brother I know,
The rest might not, but I have treasur'd every note,
For more than once dimly down to the beach gliding,
Silent, avoiding the moonbeams, blending myself with the shadows,
Recalling now the obscure shapes, the echoes, the sounds and sights after their sorts,
The white arms out in the breakers tirelessly tossing,
I, with bare feet, a child, the wind wafting my hair,
Listen'd long and long.

Listen'd to keep, to sing, now translating the notes,
Following you my brother.

Soothe! soothe! soothe!
Close on its wave soothes the wave behind,
And again another behind embracing and lapping, every one close,
But my love soothes not me, not me.

O madly the sea pushes upon the land,
With love, with love.

O night! do I not see my love fluttering out among the breakers?
What is that little black thing I see there in the white?

Loud! loud! loud!
Loud I call to you, my love!
High and clear I shoot my voice over the waves,
Surely you must know who is here, is here,
You must know who I am, my love.

Low-hanging moon!
What is that dusky spot in your brown yellow?
O it is the shape, the shape of my mate!
O moon do not keep her from me any longer.

Land! land! O land!
Whichever way I turn, O I think you could give me my mate back again if you only would,

249

For I am almost sure I see her dimly whichever
  way I look.

O rising stars!
Perhaps the one I want so much will rise, will rise
  with some of you.

O throat! O trembling throat!
Sound clearer through the atmosphere!
Pierce the woods, the earth,
Somewhere listening to catch you must be the one I
  want.

Shake out carols!
Solitary here, the night's carols!
Carols of lonesome love! death's carols!
Carols under that lagging, yellow, waning moon!
O under that moon where she droops almost down
  into the sea!
O reckless despairing carols.

But soft! sink low!
Soft! let me just murmur,
And do you wait a moment you husky-nois'd sea,
For somewhere I believe I heard my mate
  responding to me,
So faint, I must be still, be still to listen,
But not altogether still, for then she might not come
  immediately to me.

Hither my love!
Here I am! here!

With this just-sustain'd note I announce myself to
* you,*
This gentle call is for you my love, for you.

Do not be decoy'd elsewhere,
That is the whistle of the wind, it is not my voice,
That is the fluttering, the fluttering of the spray,
Those are the shadows of leaves.

O darkness! O in vain!
O I am very sick and sorrowful.

O brown halo in the sky near the moon, drooping
* upon the sea!*
O troubled reflection in the sea!
O throat! O throbbing heart!
And I singing uselessly, uselessly all the night.

O past! O happy life! O songs of joy!
In the air, in the woods, over fields,
Loved! loved! loved! loved! loved!
But my mate no more, no more with me!
We two together no more.

The aria sinking,
All else continuing, the stars shining,
The winds blowing, the notes of the bird
  continuous echoing,
With angry moans the fierce old mother
  incessantly moaning,
On the sands of Paumanok's shore gray and
  rustling,

The yellow half-moon enlarged, sagging down,
  drooping, the face of the sea almost touching,
The boy ecstatic, with his bare feet the waves,
  with his hair the atmosphere dallying,
The love in the heart long pent, now loose, now
  at last tumultuously bursting,
The aria's meaning, the ears, the soul, swiftly
  depositing,
The strange tears down the cheeks coursing,
The colloquy there, the trio, each uttering,
The undertone, the savage old mother
  incessantly crying,
To the boy's soul's questions sullenly timing,
  some drown'd secret hissing,
To the outsetting bard.

Demon or bird! (said the boy's soul,)
Is it indeed toward your mate you sing? or is it
  really to me?
For I, that was a child, my tongue's use
  sleeping, now I have heard you,
Now in a moment I know what I am for, I
  awake,
And already a thousand singers, a thousand
  songs, clearer, louder and more sorrowful
    than yours,
A thousand warbling echoes have started to life
  within me, never to die.

O you singer solitary, singing by yourself,
  projecting me,

O solitary me listening, never more shall I cease
    perpetuating you,
Never more shall I escape, never more the
    reverberations,
Never more the cries of unsatisfied love be
    absent from me,
Never again leave me to be the peaceful child I
    was before what there in the night,
By the sea under the yellow and sagging moon,
The messenger there arous'd, the fire, the sweet
    hell within,
The unknown want, the destiny of me.

O give me the clew! (it lurks in the night here
    somewhere,)
O if I am to have so much, let me have more!

A word then, (for I will conquer it,)
The word final, superior to all,
Subtle, sent up—what is it?—I listen;
Are you whispering it, and have been all the
    time, you sea-waves?
Is that it from your liquid rims and wet sands?

Whereto answering, the sea,
Delaying not, hurrying not,
Whisper'd me through the night, and very
    plainly before daybreak,
Lisp'd to me the low and delicious word death,
And again death, death, death, death,
Hissing melodious, neither like the bird nor like
    my arous'd child's heart,

But edging near as privately for me rustling at
　　my feet,
Creeping thence steadily up to my ears and
　　laving me softly all over,
Death, death, death, death, death.

Which I do not forget,
But fuse the song of my dusky demon and
　　brother,
That he sang to me in the moonlight on
　　Paumanok's gray beach,
With the thousand responsive songs at random,
My own songs awaked from that hour,
And with them the key, the word up from the
　　waves,
The word of the sweetest song and all songs,
That strong and delicious word which, creeping
　　to my feet,
(Or like some old crone rocking the cradle,
　　swathed in sweet garments, bending aside,)
The sea whisper'd me.

The World below the Brine

The world below the brine,
Forests at the bottom of the sea, the branches
　　and leaves,
Sea-lettuce, vast lichens, strange flowers and
　　seeds, the thick tangle, openings, and pink
　　turf,

Different colors, pale gray and green, purple,
　　white, and gold, the play of light through the
　　　water,
Dumb swimmers there among the rocks, coral,
　　gluten, grass, rushes, and the aliment of the
　　　swimmers,
Sluggish existences grazing there suspended, or
　　slowly crawling close to the bottom,
The sperm-whale at the surface blowing air and
　　spray, or disporting with his flukes,
The leaden-eyed shark, the walrus, the turtle,
　　the hairy sea-leopard, and the sting-ray,
Passions there, wars, pursuits, tribes, sight in
　　those ocean-depths, breathing that thick-
　　　breathing air, as so many do,
The change thence to the sight here, and to the
　　subtle air breathed by beings like us who
　　　walk this sphere,
The change onward from ours to that of beings
　　who walk other spheres.

Poems by
Dante Gabriel Rossetti

Silent Noon

Your hands lie open in the long fresh grass—
 The finger-points look through like rosy
    blooms:
 Your eyes smile peace. The pasture gleams
    and glooms
'Neath billowing skies that scatter and amass.
All round our nest, far as the eye can pass,
 Are golden kingcup-fields with silver edge
 Where the cow-parsley skirts the hawthorn-
    hedge.
'Tis visible silence, still as the hour-glass.

Deep in the sun-searched growths the dragonfly
Hangs like a blue thread loosened from the sky:
 So this winged hour is dropt to us from
    above.
Oh! clasp we to our hearts, for deathless dower,
This close-companioned inarticulate hour
 When twofold silence was the song of love.

The Hill Summit

This feast-day of the sun, his altar there
 In the broad west has blazed for vesper-song;
 And I have loitered in the vale too long
And gaze now a belated worshipper.

259

Yet may I not forget that I was 'ware,
  So journeying, of his face at intervals
  Transfigured where the fringed horizon falls,
A fiery bush with coruscating hair.

And now that I have climbed and won this
      height,
  I must tread downward through the sloping
      shade
And travel the bewildered tracks till night.
  Yet for this hour I still may here be stayed
  And see the gold air and the silver fade
And the last bird fly into the last night.

The One Hope

When vain desire at last and vain regret
  Go hand in hand to death, and all is vain,
  What shall assuage the unforgotten pain
And teach the unforgetful to forget?
Shall Peace be still a sunk stream long unmet—
  Or may the soul at once in a green plain
  Stoop through the spray of some sweet life-
      fountain
And cull the dew-drenched flowering amulet?
Ah! when the wan soul in that golden air
  Between the scriptured petals softly blown
  Peers breathless for the gift of grace
      unknown,
Ah! let none other alien spell soe'er

But only the one Hope's one name be there—
   Not less nor more, but even that word alone.

The Woodspurge

The wind flapped loose, the wind was still,
Shaken out dead from tree and hill:
I had walked on at the wind's will—
I sat now, for the wind was still.

Between my knees my forehead was—
My lips, drawn in, said not Alas!
My hair was over in the grass,
My naked ears heard the day pass.

My eyes, wide open, had the run
Of some ten weeds to fix upon;
Among those few, out of the sun,
The woodspurge flowered, three cups in one.

From perfect grief there need not be
Wisdom or even memory:
One thing then learnt remains to me—
The woodspurge has a cup of three.

Poems by
Emily Dickinson

I'm Nobody
(288)

I'm Nobody! Who are you?
Are you—Nobody—Too?
Then there's a pair of us?
Don't tell! they'd advertise—you know!

How dreary—to be—Somebody!
How public—like a Frog—
To tell one's name—the livelong June—
To an admiring Bog!

A Loss of Something Ever Felt
(959)

A loss of something ever felt I—
The first that I could recollect
Bereft I was—of what I knew not
Too young that any should suspect

A Mourner walked among the children
I notwithstanding went about
As one bemoaning a Dominion
Itself the only Prince cast out—

Elder, Today, a session wiser
And fainter, too, as Wiseness is—

I find myself still softly searching
For my Delinquent Palaces—

And a Suspicion, like a Finger
Touches my Forehead now and then
That I am looking oppositely
For the site of the Kingdom of Heaven—

Wild Nights
(249)

Wild Nights—Wild Nights!
Were I with thee
Wild Nights should be
Our luxury!

Futile—the Winds—
To a Heart in port—
Done with the Compass—
Done with the Chart!

Rowing in Eden—
Ah, the Sea!
Might I but moor—Tonight—
In Thee!

If Recollecting Were Forgetting
(33)

If recollecting were forgetting,
Then I remember not.
And if forgetting, recollecting,
How near I had forgot.
And if to miss, were merry,
And to mourn, were gay,
How very blithe the fingers
That gathered this, Today!

Tell All the Truth but Tell It Slant
(1129)

Tell all the Truth but tell it slant—
Success in Circuit lies
Too bright for our infirm Delight
The Truth's superb surprise

As Lightning to the Children eased
With explanation kind
The Truth must dazzle gradually
Or every man be blind—

Much Madness Is Divinest Sense
(435)

Much Madness is divinest Sense—
To a discerning Eye—

Much Sense—the starkest Madness—
'Tis the Majority
In this, as All, prevail—
Assent—and you are sane—
Demur—you're straightway dangerous—
And handled with a Chain—

Poems by
Christina Rossetti

Echo

Come to me in the silence of the night;
  Come in the speaking silence of a dream;
Come with soft rounded cheeks and eyes as
      bright
  As sunlight on a stream;
    Come back in tears,
O memory, hope, love of finished years.

Oh dream how sweet, too sweet, too bitter
      sweet,
  Whose wakening should have been in
      Paradise,
Where souls brimful of love abide and meet;
  Where thirsting longing eyes
    Watch the slow door
That opening, letting in, lets out no more.

Yet come to me in dreams, that I may live
  My very life again tho' cold in death:
Come back to me in dreams, that I may give
  Pulse for pulse, breath for breath:
    Speak low, lean low,
As long ago, my love, how long ago.

Passing Away, Saith the World, Passing Away

Passing away, saith the World, passing away:
Chances, beauty and youth sapped day by day:
Thy life never continueth in one stay.
Is the eye waxen dim, is the dark hair changing
    to gray
That hath won neither laurel nor bay.
I shall clothe myself in Spring and bud in May:
Thou, root-stricken, shalt not rebuild thy decay
On my bosom for aye.
Then I answered: Yea.

Passing away, saith my Soul, passing away:
With its burden of fear and hope, of labor and
    play;
Hearken what the past doth witness and say:
Rust in thy gold, a moth is in thine array,
A canker is in thy bud, thy leaf must decay.
At midnight, at cockcrow, at morning, one
    certain day
Lo the bridegroom shall come and shall not
    delay:
Watch thou and pray.
Then I answered: Yea.

Passing away, saith my God, passing away:
Winter passeth after the long delay:
New grapes on the vine, new figs on the tender
    spray,
Turtle calleth turtle in Heaven's May.

Tho' I tarry, wait for Me, trust Me, watch and
   pray.
Arise, come away, night is past and lo it is day,
My love, My sister, My spouse, thou shalt hear
   Me say.
Then I answered: Yea.

Shut Out

The door was shut. I looked between
   Its iron bars; and saw it lie,
   My garden, mine, beneath the sky,
Pied with all flowers bedewed and green:

From bough to bough the song-birds crossed,
   From flower to flower the moths and bees;
   With all its nests and stately trees
It had been mine, and it was lost.

A shadowless spirit kept the gate,
   Blank and unchanging like the grave.
   I peering thro' said: "Let me have
Some buds to cheer my outcast state."

He answered not. "Or give me, then,
   But one small twig from shrub or tree;
   And bid my home remember me
Until I come to it again."

The spirit was silent; but he took
   Mortar and stone to build a wall;

He left no loophole great or small
Thro' which my straining eyes might look:

So now I sit here quite alone
    Blinded with tears; nor grieve for that,
    For nought is left worth looking at
Since my delightful land is gone.

A violet bed is budding near,
    Wherein a lark has made her nest:
    And good they are, but not the best;
And dear they are, but not so dear.

The Convent Threshold

There's blood between us, love, my love,
There's father's blood, there's brother's blood;
And blood's a bar I cannot pass:
I choose the stairs that mount above,
Stair after golden skyward stair,
To city and to sea of glass.
My lily feet are soiled with mud,
With scarlet mud which tells a tale
Of hope that was, of guilt that was,
Of love that shall not yet avail;
Alas, my heart, if I could bare
My heart, this selfsame stain is there:
I seek the sea of glass and fire
To wash the spot, to burn the snare;
Lo, stairs are meant to lift us higher:
Mount with me, mount the kindled stair.

Your eyes look earthward, mine look up.
I see the far-off city grand,
Beyond the hills a watered land,
Beyond the gulf a gleaming strand
Of mansions where the righteous sup;
Who sleep at ease among their trees,
Or wake to sing a cadenced hymn
With Cherubim and Seraphim:
They bore the Cross, they drained the cup,
Racked, roasted, crushed, wrenched limb from
    limb,
They the offscouring of the world:
The heaven of starry heavens unfurled,
The sun before their face is dim.

You looking earthward, what see you?
Milk-white, wine-flushed among the vines,
Up and down leaping, to and fro,
Most glad, most full, made strong with wines,
Blooming as peaches pearled with dew,
Their golden windy hair afloat,
Love-music warbling in their throat,
Young men and women come and go.

You linger, yet the time is short:
Flee for your life, gird up your strength
To flee; the shadows stretched at length
Show that day wanes, that night draws nigh;
Flee to the mountain, tarry not.
Is this a time for smile and sigh,
For songs among the secret trees
Where sudden blue birds nest and sport?

The time is short and yet you stay:
Today while it is called today
Kneel, wrestle, knock, do violence, pray;
Today is short, tomorrow nigh:
Why will you die? why will you die?

You sinned with me a pleasant sin:
Repent with me, for I repent.
Woe's me the lore I must unlearn!
Woe's me that easy way we went,
So rugged when I would return!
How long until my sleep begin,
How long shall stretch these nights and days?
Surely, clean Angels cry, she prays;
She laves her soul with tedious tears:
How long must stretch these years and years?

I turn from you my cheeks and eyes,
My hair which you shall see no more—
Alas for joy that went before,
For joy that dies, for love that dies.
Only my lips still turn to you,
My livid lips that cry, Repent.
Oh weary life, Oh weary Lent,
Oh weary time whose stars are few.

How should I rest in Paradise,
Or sit on steps of heaven alone?
If Saints and Angels spoke of love
Should I not answer from my throne:
Have pity upon me, ye my friends,

For I have heard the sound thereof:
Should I not turn with yearning eyes,
Turn earthwards with a pitiful pang?
Oh save me from a pang in heaven.
By all the gifts we took and gave,
Repent, repent, and be forgiven:
This life is long, but yet it ends;
Repent and purge your soul and save:
No gladder song the morning stars
Upon their birthday morning sang
Than Angels sing when one repents.

I tell you what I dreamed last night:
A spirit with transfigured face
Fire-footed clomb an infinite space.
I heard his hundred pinions clang,
Heaven-bells rejoicing rang and rang,
Heaven-air was thrilled with subtle scents,
Worlds spun upon their rushing cars:
He mounted shrieking: "Give me light."
Still light was poured on him, more light;
Angels, Archangels he outstripped
Exultant in exceeding might,
And trod the skirts of Cherubim.
Still "Give me light," he shrieked; and dipped
His thirsty face, and drank a sea,
Athirst with thirst it could not slake.
I saw him, drunk with knowledge, take
From aching brows the aureole crown—
His locks writhed like a cloven snake—
He left his throne to grovel down
And lick the dust of Seraphs' feet:

For what is knowledge duly weighed?
Knowledge is strong, but love is sweet;
Yea all the progress he had made
Was but to learn that all is small
Save love, for love is all in all.

I tell you what I dreamed last night:
It was not dark, it was not light,
Cold dews had drenched my plenteous hair
Thro' clay; you came to seek me there.
And "Do you dream of me?" you said.
My heart was dust that used to leap
To you; I answered half asleep:
"My pillow is damp, my sheets are red,
There's a leaden tester to my bed:
Find you a warmer playfellow,
A warmer pillow for your head,
A kinder love to love than mine."
You wrung your hands; while I like lead
Crushed downwards thro' the sodden earth:
You smote your hands but not in mirth,
And reeled but were not drunk with wine.

For all night long I dreamed of you:
I woke and prayed against my will,
Then slept to dream of you again.
At length I rose and knelt and prayed:
I cannot write the words I said,
My words were slow, my tears were few;
But thro' the dark my silence spoke
Like thunder. When this morning broke,
My face was pinched, my hair was gray,

And frozen blood was on the sill
Where stifling in my struggle I lay.

If now you saw me you would say:
Where is the face I used to love?
And I would answer: Gone before;
It tarries veiled in paradise.
When once the morning star shall rise,
When earth with shadow flees away
And we stand safe within the door,
Then you shall lift the veil thereof.
Look up, rise up: for far above
Our palms are grown, our place is set;
There we shall meet as once we met
And love with old familiar love.

Poems by
Lewis Carroll

The Lobster Quadrille
(from *Alice's Adventures in Wonderland*)

"Will you walk a little faster?" said a whiting to
    a snail,
"There's a porpoise close behind us, and he's
    treading on my tail.
See how eagerly the lobsters and the turtles all
    advance!
They are waiting on the shingle—will you come
    and join the dance?
  Will you, wo'n't you, will you, wo'n't you,
    will you join the dance?
  Will you, wo'n't you, will you, wo'n't you,
    wo'n't you join the dance?

"You can really have no notion how delightful it
    will be
When they take us up and throw us, with the
    lobsters, out to sea!"
But the snail replied "Too far, too far!", and
    gave a look askance—
Said he thanked the whiting kindly, but he
    would not join the dance.
  Would not, could not, would not, could not,
    could not join the dance.
  Would not, could not, would not, could not,
    could not join the dance.

"What matters it how far we go?" his scaly
    friend replied.
"There is another shore, you know, upon the
    other side.
The further off from England the nearer is to
    France.
Then turn not pale, beloved snail, but come and
    join the dance.
    Will you, wo'n't you, will you, wo'n't you,
        will you join the dance?
    Will you, wo'n't you, will you, wo'n't you,
        wo'n't you join the dance?"

Solitude

I love the stillness of the wood:
    I love the music of the rill:
I love to couch in pensive mood
    Upon some silent hill.

Scarce heard, beneath yon arching trees,
    The silver-crested ripples pass;
And, like a mimic brook, the breeze
    Whispers among the grass.

Here from the world I win release,
    Nor scorn of men, nor footstep rude,
Break in to mar the holy peace
    Of this great solitude.

Here may the silent tears I weep
  Lull the vexed spirit into rest,
As infants sob themselves to sleep
  Upon a mother's breast.

But when the bitter hour is gone,
  And the keen throbbing pangs are
  still,
Oh, sweetest then to couch alone
  Upon some silent hill!

To live in joys that once have been,
  To put the cold world out of sight,
And deck life's drear and barren scene
  With hues of rainbow-light.

For what to man the gift of breath,
  If sorrow be his lot below;
If all the day that ends in death
  Be dark with clouds of woe?

Shall the poor transport of an hour
  Repay long years of sore distress—
The fragrance of a lonely flower
  Make glad the wilderness?

Ye golden hours of Life's young spring,
  Of innocence, of love and truth!
Bright, beyond all imagining,
  Thou fairy-dream of youth!

I'd give all wealth that years have piled,
 The slow result of Life's decay,
To be once more a little child
 For one bright summer-day.

Alice's Evidence
(from *Alice's Adventures in Wonderland*)

"They told me you had been to her,
 And mentioned me to him:
She gave me a good character,
But said I could not swim.

He sent them word I had not gone
 (We know it to be true):
If she should push the matter on,
 What would become of you?

I gave her one, they gave him two,
 You gave us three or more;
They all returned from him to you,
 Though they were mine before.

If I or she should chance to be
 Involved in this affair,
He trusts to you to set them free,
 Exactly as we were.

My notion was that you had been
   (Before she had this fit)
An obstacle that came between
   Him, and ourselves, and it.

Don't let him know she liked them best,
   For this must ever be
A secret, kept from all the rest.
   Between yourself and me."

Poems by
Thomas Hardy

The Voice

Woman much missed, how you call to me,
    call to me,
Saying that now you are not as you were
When you had changed from the one who
    was all to me,
But as at first, when our day was fair.

Can it be you that I hear? Let me view you,
    then,
Standing as when I drew near to the town
Where you would wait for me: yes, as I
    knew you then,
Even to the original air-blue gown!

Or is it only the breeze, in its listlessness
Traveling across the wet mead to me here,
You being ever dissolved to wan
    wistlessness,
Heard no more again far or near?

    Thus I; faltering forward,
    Leaves around me falling,
Wind oozing thin through the thorn from
    norward,
    And the woman calling.

The Convergence of the Twain

LINES ON THE LOSS OF THE TITANIC

1

In a solitude of the sea
Deep from human vanity,
And the Pride of Life that planned her, stilly
  couches she.

2

Steel chambers, late the pyres
Of her salamandrine fires,
Cold currents thrid, and turn to rhythmic tidal
  lyres.

3

Over the mirrors meant
To glass the opulent
The sea-worm crawls—grotesque, slimed,
  dumb, indifferent.

4

Jewels in joy designed
To ravish the sensuous mind
Lie lightless, all their sparkles bleared and
  black and blind.

5

Dim moon-eyed fishes near
Gaze at the gilded gear
And query: "What does this vaingloriousness
   down here?"

6

Well: while was fashioning
This creature of cleaving wing,
The Immanent Will that stirs and urges
   everything

7

Prepared a sinister mate
For her—so gaily great—
A Shape of Ice, for the time far and dissociate.

8

And as the smart ship grew
In stature, grace, and hue,
In shadowy silent distance grew the Iceberg
   too.

9

Alien they seemed to be:
No mortal eye could see
The intimate welding of their later history,

10
Or sign that they were bent
By paths coincident
On being anon twin halves of one august
    event,

11
Till the Spinner of the Years
Said "Now!" And each one hears,
And consummation comes, and jars two
    hemispheres.

Nature's Questioning

When I look forth at dawning, pool,
    Field, flock, and lonely tree,
    All seem to gaze at me
Like chastened children sitting silent in a
    school;

Their faces dulled, constrained, and worn,
    As though the master's way
    Through the long teaching day
Had cowed them till their early zest was
    overborne.

Upon them stirs in lippings mere
    (As if once clear in call,
    But now scarce breathed at all)—
'We wonder, ever wonder, why we find us here!

'Has some Vast Imbecility,
    Mighty to build and blend,
    But impotent to tend,
Framed us in jest, and left us now to hazardry?

'Or come we of an Automaton
    Unconscious of our pains? . . .
    Or are we live remains
Of Godhead dying downwards, brain and eye
        now gone?

Or is it that some high Plan betides,
    As yet not understood,
    Of Evil stormed by Good,
We the Forlorn Hope over which Achievement
        strides?'

Thus things around. No answerer I. . . .
    Meanwhile the winds, and rains,
    And Earth's old glooms and pains
Are still the same, and Life and Death are
        neighbours nigh.

Poems by
Gerard Manley Hopkins

The Windhover

TO CHRIST OUR LORD

I caught this morning morning's minion, king-
    dom of daylight's dauphin, dapple-dawn-
    drawn Falcon, in his riding
  Of the rolling level underneath him steady
    air, and striding
High there, how he rung upon the rein of a
    wimpling wing
In his ecstasy! then off, off forth on swing,
  As a skate's heel sweeps smooth on a bow-
    bend: the hurl and gliding
  Rebuffed the big wind. My heart in hiding
Stirred for a bird,—the achieve of, the mastery
    of the thing!

Brute beauty and valour and act, oh, air, pride,
    plume, here
  Buckle! AND the fire that breaks from thee
    then, a billion
Times told lovelier, more dangerous, O my
    chevalier!

  No wonder of it: shéer plód makes plough
    down sillion
Shine, and blue-bleak embers, ah my dear,
  Fall, gall themselves, and gash gold-vermilion.

299

Pied Beauty

Glory be to God for dappled things—
   For skies of couple-colour as a brinded
      cow;
     For rose-moles all in stipple upon trout
      that swim;
Fresh-firecoal chestnut-falls; finches wings;
   Landscape plotted and pieced—fold, fallow,
      and plough;
     And áll trádes, their gear and tackle and
      trim.
All things counter, original, spare, strange;
   Whatever is fickle, freckled (who knows
      how?)
     With swift, slow; sweet, sour; adazzle, dim;
He fathers-forth whose beauty is past change:
                    Praise him.

Spring and Fall

TO A YOUNG CHILD

Márgarét, áre you gríeving
Over Goldengrove unleaving?
Leáves, líke the things of man, you
With your fresh thoughts care for, can you?
Áh! ás the heart grows older
It will come to such sights colder
By and by, nor spare a sigh
Though worlds of wanwood leafmeal lie;

And yet you *will* weep and know why.
Now no matter, child, the name:
Sórrow's springs áre the same.
Nor mouth had, no nor mind, expressed
What heart heard of, ghost guessed:
It ís the blight man was born for,
It is Margaret you mourn for.

Poems by
James Whitcomb
Riley

Knee-Deep in June

Tell you what I like the best—
   'Long about knee-deep in June,
'Bout the time strawberries melts
   On the vine,—some afternoon
Like to jes' git out and rest,
   And not work at nothin' else!

Orchard's where I'd ruther be—
Needn't fence it in for me!—
   Jes' the whole sky overhead,
And the whole airth underneath—
Sorto' so's a man kin breathe
   Like he ort, and kindo' has
Elbow room to keerlessly
     Sprawl out len'thways on the grass
       Where the shadders thick and soft
     As the kivvers on the bed
      Mother fixes in the loft
Allus, when they's company!

Jes' a-sorto' lazin' there—
   S'lazy, 'at you peek and peer
      Through the wavin' leaves above,
      Like a feller 'at's in love
     And don't know it, ner don't keer!
Ever'thing you hear and see
      Got some sorto' interest—

Maybe find a bluebird's nest
Tucked up there conveenently
Fer the boy 'at's ap' to be
Up some other apple-tree!
Watch the swallers skootin' past
'Bout as peert as you could ast;
    Er the Bob-white raise and whiz
    Where some other's whistle is.

Ketch a shadder down below,
And look up to find the crow—
Er a hawk—away up there,
'Peerantly froze in the air!—
    Hear the old hen squawk, and squat
    Over ever' chick she's got,
Suddent-like—and she knows where
    That-air hawk is, well as you!—
    You jes' bet yer life she do!—
        Eyes a-glitterin' like glass,
        Waitin' till he makes a pass!

Pee-wees' singin', to express
    My opinion, 's second class,
Yit you'll hear 'em more er less;
    Sapsucks gittin' down to biz,
Weedin' out the lonesomeness;
    Mr. Bluejay, full o' sass,
        In them base-ball clothes o' his,
Sportin' round the orchard jes'
Like he owned the premises!
    Sun out in the fields kin sizz,

But flat on yer back, I guess,
    In the shade 's where glory is!
That's jes' what I'd like to do
Stiddy fer a year er two!

Plague! ef they ain't somepin' in
Work 'at kindo' goes ag'in
    My convictions!—'long about
      Here in June especially!—
      Under some old apple-tree,
        Jes' a-restin' through and through,
I could git along without
      Nothin' else at all to do
      Only jes' a-wishin' you
    Wuz a-gittin' there like me,
    And June was eternity!

Lay out there and try to see
Jes' how lazy you kin be!—
    Tumble round and souse yer head
      In the clover-bloom, er pull
    Yer straw hat acrost yer eyes
    And peek through it at the skies,
Thinkin' of old chums 'at's dead;
    Maybe smilin' back at you
      I' betwixt the beautiful
    Clouds o' gold and white and blue!—
Month a man kin railly love—
June, you know, I'm talkin' of!

March ain't never nothin' new!—
Aprile's altogether too

Brash fer me! and May—I jes'
'Bominate its promises,—
Little hints o' sunshine and
Green around the timber-land—
    A few promises, and a few
    Chip-birds, and a sprout er two,—
        Drap asleep, and it turns in
        'Fore daylight and snows ag'in!—

But when June comes—Clear my throat
    With wild honey!—Rench my hair
In the dew! and hold my coat!
        Whoop out loud! and throw my hat!—
June wants me, and I'm to spare!
Spread them shadders anywhere,
I'll git down and waller there,
        And obleeged to you at that!

Out to Old Aunt Mary's

Wasn't it pleasant, O brother mine,
In those old days of the lost sunshine
    Of youth—when the Saturday's chores were
            through,
    And the "Sunday's wood" in the kitchen,
            too,
    And we went visiting, "me and you,"
        Out to Old Aunt Mary's?

It all comes back so clear today!
Though I am as bald as you are gray—

Out by the barn-lot, and down the lane,
We patter along in the dust again,
As light as the tips of the drops of the rain,
    Out to Old Aunt Mary's!

We cross the pasture, and through the wood
Where the old gray snag of the poplar stood,
    Where the hammering red-heads hopped
        awry,
    And the buzzard "raised" in the clearing sky,
    And lolled and circled, as we went by,
    Out to Old Aunt Mary's.

And then in the dust of the road again;
And the teams we met, and the countrymen;
    And the long highway, with sunshine spread
    As thick as butter on country bread,
    Our cares behind, and our hearts ahead
    Out to Old Aunt Mary's.

Why, I see her now in the open door,
Where the little gourds grew up the sides, and
        o'er
    The clapboard roof!—And her face—ah, me!
    Wasn't it good for a boy to see—
    And wasn't it good for a boy to be
    Out to Old Aunt Mary's?

The jelly—the jam and the marmalade,
And the cherry and quince "preserves" she
        made!

And the sweet-sour pickles of peach and pear,
With cinnamon in 'em, and all things rare!—
And the more we ate was the more to spare,
    Out to Old Aunt Mary's!

And the old spring-house in the cool green
        gloom
Of the willow-trees, and the cooler room
    Where the swinging-shelves and the crocks
        were kept—
    Where the cream in a golden languor slept
    While the waters gurgled and laughed and
        wept—
    Out to Old Aunt Mary's!

And as many a time have you and I—
Barefoot boys in the days gone by—
    Knelt, and in tremulous ecstasies
    Dipped our lips into sweets like these,—
    Memory now is on her knees
    Out to Old Aunt Mary's!

And O, my brother, so far away,
This is to tell you she waits *today*
    To welcome us:—Aunt Mary fell
    Asleep this morning, whispering, "Tell
    The boys to come!" And all is well
    Out to Old Aunt Mary's!

Poems by
Robert Louis
Stevenson

My Shadow

I have a little shadow that goes in and out
  with me,
And what can be the use of him is more
  than I can see.
He is very, very like me from the heels up
  to the head;
And I see him jump before me, when I
  jump into my bed.

The funniest thing about him is the way he
  likes to grow—
Not at all like proper children, which is
  always very slow;
For he sometimes shoots up taller like an
  india-rubber ball,
And he sometimes gets so little that there's
  none of him at all.

He hasn't got a notion of how children
  ought to play,
And can only make a fool of me in every
  sort of way.
He stays so close beside me, he's a coward
  you can see;
I'd think shame to stick to nursie as that
  shadow sticks to me!

One morning, very early, before the sun was
    up,
I rose and found the shining dew on every
    buttercup;
But my lazy little shadow, like an arrant
    sleepy-head,
Had stayed at home behind me and was fast
    asleep in bed.

Bed in Summer

In winter I get up at night
And dress by yellow candle-light.
In summer, quite the other way,
I have to go to bed by day.

I have to go to bed and see
The birds still hopping on the tree,
Or hear the grown-up people's feet
Still going past me in the street.

And does it not seem hard to you,
When all the sky is clear and blue,
And I should like so much to play,
To have to go to bed by day?

Youth and Love

Once only by the garden gate
  Our lips we joined and parted.

I must fulfil an empty fate
    And travel the uncharted.

Hail and farewell! I must arise,
    Leave here the fatted cattle,
And paint on foreign lands and skies
    My Odyssey of battle.

The untented Kosmos my abode,
    I pass, a wilful stranger:
My mistress still the open road
    And the bright eyes of danger.

Come ill or well, the cross, the crown,
    The rainbow or the thunder,
I fling my soul and body down
    For God to plough them under.

Foreign Lands

Up into the cherry-tree
Who should climb but little me?
I held the trunk with both my hands
And looked abroad on foreign lands.

I saw the next-door garden lie,
Adorned with flowers, before my eye,
And many pleasant places more
That I had never seen before.

I saw the dimpling river pass
And be the sky's blue looking-glass;
The dusty roads go up and down
With people tramping in to town.

If I could find a higher tree,
Farther and farther I should see,
To where the grown-up river slips
Into the sea among the ships,

To where the roads on either hand
Lead onward into fairy land,
Where all the children dine at five,
And all the playthings come alive.

Poems by
Rudyard Kipling

Tommy

I went into a public-'ouse to get a pint o' beer,
The publican 'e up an' sez, "We serve no red-
      coats here."
The girls be'ind the bar they laughed an'
      giggled fit to die,
I outs into the street again an' to myself sez I:
      O it's Tommy this, an' Tommy that, an'
      "Tommy, go away";
      But it's "Thank you, Mister Atkins," when
      the band begins to play—
      The band begins to play, my boys, the
      band begins to play,
      O it's "Thank you, Mister Atkins," when
      the band begins to play.

I went into a theater as sober as could be,
They gave a drunk civilian room, but 'adn't
      none for me;
They sent me to the gallery or round the music-
      'alls,
But when it comes to fightin', Lord! they'll
      shove me in the stalls!
      For it's Tommy this, an' Tommy that, an'
      "Tommy, wait outside";
      But it's "Special train for Atkins" when the
      trooper's on the tide—

The troopship's on the tide, my boys, the
    troopship's on the tide,
  O it's "Special train for Atkins" when the
    trooper's on the tide.

Yes, makin' mock o' uniforms that guard you
    while you sleep
Is cheaper than them uniforms, an' they're
    starvation cheap;
An' hustlin' drunken soldiers when they're goin'
    large a bit
Is five times better business than paradin' in full
    kit.
    Then it's Tommy this, an' Tommy that,
    an' "Tommy, 'ow's yer soul?"
    But it's "Thin red line of 'eroes" when the
    drums begin to roll—
    The drums begin to roll, my boys, the
    drums begin to roll,
    O it's "Thin red line of 'eroes" when the
    drums begin to roll.

We aren't no thin red 'eroes, nor we aren't no
    blackguards too,
But single men in barricks, most remarkable
    like you;
An' if sometimes our conduck isn't all your
    fancy paints,
Why, single men in barricks don't grow into
    plaster saints;
    While it's Tommy this, an' Tommy that,
    an' "Tommy, fall be'ind,"

But it's "Please to walk in front, sir," when
    there's trouble in the wind—
There's trouble in the wind, my boys,
    there's trouble in the wind,
O it's "Please to walk in front, sir," when
    there's trouble in the wind.

You talk o' better food for us, an' schools, an'
    fires, an' all:
We'll wait for extry rations if you treat us
    rational.
Don't mess about the cook-room slops, but
    prove it to our face
The Widow's Uniform is not the soldier-man's
    disgrace.
    For it's Tommy this, an' Tommy that, an'
      "Chuck him out, the brute!"
    But it's "Savior of 'is country" when the
      guns begin to shoot;
    An' it's Tommy this, an' Tommy that, an'
      anything you please;
    An' Tommy ain't a bloomin' fool—you bet
      that Tommy sees!

The Way Through the Woods

They shut the road through the woods
Seventy years ago.
Weather and rain have undone it again,
And now you would never know
There was once a road through the woods

321

Before they planted the trees.
It is underneath the coppice and heath
And the thin anemones.
Only the keeper sees
That, where the ring-dove broods,
And the badgers roll at ease,
There was once a road through the woods.

Yet, if you enter the woods
Of a summer evening late,
When the night-air cools on the trout-ringed
    pools
Where the otter whistles his mate,
(They fear not men in the woods,
Because they see so few.)
You will hear the beat of a horse's feet,
And the swish of a skirt in the dew,
Steadily cantering through
The misty solitudes,
As though they perfectly knew
The old lost road through the woods. . . .
But there is no road through the woods.

Poems by
William Butler
Yeats

The Song of Wandering Aengus

I went out to the hazel wood,
Because a fire was in my head,
And cut and peeled a hazel wand,
And hooked a berry to a thread;
And when white moths were on the wing,
And moth-like stars were flickering out,
I dropped the berry in a stream
And caught a little silver trout.

When I had laid it on the floor
I went to blow the fire aflame,
But something rustled on the floor,
And some one called me by my name:
It had become a glimmering girl
With apple blossom in her hair
Who called me by my name and ran
And faded through the brightening air.

Though I am old with wandering
Through hollow lands and hilly lands,
I will find out where she has gone,
And kiss her lips and take her hands;
And walk among long dappled grass,
And pluck till time and times are done
The silver apples of the moon,
The golden apples of the sun.

Adam's Curse

We sat together at one summer's end,
That beautiful mild woman, your close friend,
And you and I, and talked of poetry.
I said, "A line will take us hours maybe;
Yet if it does not seem a moment's thought,
Our stitching and unstitching has been naught.
Better go down upon your marrow-bones
And scrub a kitchen pavement, or break stones
Like an old pauper, in all kinds of weather;
For to articulate sweet sounds together
Is to work harder than all these, and yet
Be thought an idler by the noisy set
Of bankers, schoolmasters, and clergymen
The martyrs call the world."

                    And thereupon
That beautiful mild woman for whose sake
There's many a one shall find out all heartache
On finding that her voice is sweet and low
Replied, "To be born woman is to know—
Although they do not talk of it at school—
That we must labor to be beautiful."

I said, "It's certain there is no fine thing
Since Adam's fall but needs much laboring.
There have been lovers who thought love should
    be
So much compounded of high courtesy
That they would sigh and quote with learned
    looks

326

Precedents out of beautiful old books;
Yet now it seems an idle trade enough."

We sat grown quiet at the name of love;
We saw the last embers of daylight die,
And in the trembling blue-green of the sky
A moon, worn as if it had been a shell
Washed by time's waters as they rose and fell
About the stars and broke in days and years.

I had a thought for no one's but your ears:
That you were beautiful, and that I strove
To love you in the old high way of love;
That it had all seemed happy, and yet we'd
    grown
As weary-hearted as that hollow moon.

The Wild Swans at Coole

The trees are in their autumn beauty,
The woodland paths are dry,
Under the October twilight the water
Mirrors a still sky;
Upon the brimming water among the stones
Are nine-and-fifty swans.

The nineteenth autumn has come upon me
Since I first made my count;
I saw, before I had well finished,
All suddenly mount

And scatter wheeling in great broken rings
Upon their clamorous wings.

I have looked upon those brilliant creatures,
And now my heart is sore.
All's changed since I, hearing at twilight,
The first time on this shore,
The bell-beat of their wings above my head,
Trod with a lighter tread.

Unwearied still, lover by lover,
They paddle in the cold
Companionable streams or climb the air;
Their hearts have not grown old;
Passion or conquest, wander where they will,
Attend upon them still.

But now they drift on the still water,
Mysterious, beautiful;
Among what rushes will they build,
By what lake's edge or pool
Delight men's eyes when I awake some day
To find they have flown away?

A Deep-Sworn Vow

Others because you did not keep
That deep-sworn vow have been friends of
    mine;
Yet always when I look death in the face,
When I clamber to the heights of sleep,

Or when I grow excited with wine,
Suddenly I meet your face.

The Dawn

I would be ignorant as the dawn
That has looked down
On that old queen measuring a town
With the pin of a brooch,
Or on the withered men that saw
From their pedantic Babylon
The careless planets in their courses,
The stars fade out where the moon comes,
And took their tablets and did sums;
I would be ignorant as the dawn
That merely stood, rocking the glittering coach
Above the cloudy shoulders of the horses;
I would be—for no knowledge is worth a
    straw—
Ignorant and wanton as the dawn.

Brown Penny

I whispered, 'I am too young.'
And then, 'I am old enough';
Wherefore I threw a penny
To find out if I might love
'Go and love, go and love, young man,
If the lady be young and fair.'

Ah, penny, brown penny, brown penny,
I am looped in the loops of her hair.

O love is a crooked thing,
There is nobody wise enough
To find out all that is in it,
For he would be thinking of love
Till the stars had run away
And the shadows eaten the moon.
Ah, penny, brown penny, brown penny,
One cannot begin it too soon.

A Drinking Song

Wine comes in at the mouth
And love comes in at the eye;
That's all we shall know for truth
Before we grow old and die.
I lift the glass to my mouth,
I look at you, and I sigh.

Poems by
Edwin Arlington Robinson

New England

Here where the wind is always north-north-east
And children learn to walk on frozen toes,
Wonder begets an envy of all those
Who boil elsewhere with such a lyric yeast
Of love that you will hear them at a feast
Where demons would appeal for some repose,
Still clamoring where the chalice overflows
And crying wildest who have drunk the least.

Passion is here a soilure of the wits,
We're told, and Love a cross for them to bear;
Joy shivers in the corner where she knits
And Conscience always has the rocking-chair,
Cheerful as when she tortured into fits
The first cat that was ever killed by Care.

Reuben Bright

Because he was a butcher and thereby
Did earn an honest living (and did right),
I would not have you think that Reuben Bright
Was any more a brute than you or I;
For when they told him that his wife must die,
He stared at them, and shook with grief and
    fright,

And cried like a great baby half that night,
And made the women cry to see him cry.

And after she was dead, and he had paid
The singers and the sexton and the rest,
He packed a lot of things that she had made
Most mournfully away in an old chest
Of hers, and put some chopped-up cedar
  boughs
In with them, and tore down the slaughter-
  house.

Poems by
Walter de la Mare

Nod

Softly along the road of evening,
  In a twilight dim with rose,
Wrinkled with age, and drenched with dew,
  Old Nod, the shepherd, goes.

His drowsy flock streams on before him,
  Their fleeces charged with gold,
To where the sun's last beam leans low
  On Nod the shepherd's fold.

The hedge is quick and green with brier,
  From their sand the conies creep;
And all the birds that fly in heaven
  Flock singing home to sleep.

His lambs outnumber a noon's roses,
  Yet, when night's shadows fall,
His blind old sheep-dog, Slumber-soon,
  Misses not one of all.

His are the quiet steeps of dreamland,
  The waters of no-more-pain,
His ram's bell rings 'neath an arch of stars,
  'Rest, rest and rest again.'

Comfort

As I mused by the hearthside,
      Puss said to me:
'There burns the Fire, man,
      And here sit we.

'Four Walls around us
      Against the cold air;
And the latchet drawn close
      To the draughty Stair.

'A Roof o'er our heads
      Star-proof, moon immune,
And a wind in the chimney
      To wail us a tune.

'What Felicity!' miaowed he,
      'Where none may intrude;
Just Man and Beast—met
      In this Solitude!

'Dear God, what security,
      Comfort and bliss!
And to think, too, what ages
      Have brought us to this!

'You in your sheep's-wool coat,
      Buttons of bone,
And me in my fur-about
      On the warm hearthstone.'

Poems by
Robert Frost

The Need of Being Versed
in Country Things

The house had gone to bring again
To the midnight sky a sunset glow.
Now the chimney was all of the house that
    stood,
Like a pistil after the petals go.

The barn opposed across the way,
That would have joined the house in flame
Had it been the will of the wind, was left
To bear forsaken the place's name.

No more it opened with all one end
For teams that came by the stony road
To drum on the floor with scurrying hoofs
And brush the mow with the summer load.

The birds that came to it through the air
At broken windows flew out and in,
Their murmur more like the sigh we sigh
From too much dwelling on what has been.

Yet for them the lilac renewed its leaf,
And the aged elm, though touched with fire;
And the dry pump flung up an awkward arm;
And the fence post carried a strand of wire.

For them there was really nothing sad.
But though they rejoiced in the nest they kept,
One had to be versed in country things
Not to believe the phoebes wept.

The Aim Was Song

Before man came to blow it right
    The wind once blew itself untaught,
And did its loudest day and night
    In any rough place where it caught.

Man came to tell it what was wrong:
    It hadn't found the place to blow;
It blew too hard—the aim was song.
    And listen—how it ought to go!

He took a little in his mouth,
    And held it long enough for north
To be converted into south,
    And then by measure blew it forth.

By measure. It was word and note,
    The wind the wind had meant to be—
A little through the lips and throat.
    The aim was song—the wind could see.

Meeting and Passing

As I went down the hill along the wall
There was a gate I had leaned at for the view
And had just turned from when I first saw you
As you came up the hill. We met. But all
We did that day was mingle great and small
Footprints in summer dust as if we drew
The figure of our being less than two
But more than one as yet. Your parasol
Pointed the decimal off with one deep thrust.
And all the time we talked you seemed to see
Something down there to smile at in the dust.
(Oh, it was without prejudice to me!)
Afterward I went past what you had passed
Before we met, and you what I had passed.

Poems by
Wallace Stevens

The Brave Man

The sun, that brave man,
Comes through boughs that lie in wait,
That brave man.

Green and gloomy eyes
In dark forms of the grass
Run away.

The good stars,
Pale helms and spiky spurs,
Run away.

Fears of my bed,
Fears of life and fears of death,
Run away.

That brave man comes up
From below and walks without meditation,
That brave man.

The House Was Quiet and the World Was Calm

The house was quiet and the world was calm.
The reader became the book; and summer night

347

Was like the conscious being of the book.
The house was quiet and the world was calm.

The words were spoken as if there was no book,
Except that the reader leaned above the page,

Wanted to lean, wanted much most to be
The scholar to whom his book is true, to whom

The summer night is like a perfection of
    thought.
The house was quiet because it had to be.

The quiet was part of the meaning, part of the
    mind:
The access of perfection to the page.

And the world was calm. The truth in a calm
    world,
In which there is no other meaning, itself

Is calm, itself is summer and night, itself
Is the reader leaning late and reading there.

Poems by
Alfred Noyes

The Two Worlds

This outer world is but the pictured scroll
     Of worlds within the soul,
A coloured chart, a blazoned missal-book
     Whereon who rightly look
May spell the splendours with their mortal eyes
     And steer to Paradise.

O, well for him that knows and early knows
     In his own soul the rose
Secretly burgeons, of this earthly flower
     The heavenly paramour:
And all these fairy dreams of green-wood fern,
     These waves that break and yearn,
Shadows and hieroglyphs, hills, clouds and seas,
     Faces and flowers and trees,
Terrestrial picture-parables, relate
     Each to its heavenly mate.

O, well for him that finds in sky and sea
     This two-fold mystery,
And loses not (as painfully he spells
     The fine-spun syllables)
The cadences, the burning inner gleam,
     The poet's heavenly dream.

Well for the poet if this earthly chart
     Be printed in his heart,

351

When to his world of spirit woods and seas
    With eager face he flees
And treads the untrodden fields of unknown
       flowers
    And threads the angelic bowers,
And hears that unheard nightingale whose moan
    Trembles within his own,
And lovers murmuring in the leafy lanes
    Of his own joys and pains.

For though he voyages further than the flight
    Of earthly day and night,
Traversing to the sky's remotest ends
    A world that he transcends,
Safe, he shall hear the hidden breakers roar
    Against the mystic shore;
Shall roam the yellow sands where sirens bare
    Their breasts and wind their hair;
Shall with their perfumed tresses blind his eyes,
    And still possess the skies.

He, where the deep unearthly jungles are,
    Beneath his Eastern star
Shall pass the tawny lion in his den
    And cross the quaking fen.
He learnt his path (and treads it undefiled)
    When, as a little child,
He bent his head with long and loving looks
    O'er earthly picture-books.
His earthly love nestles against his side,
    His young celestial guide.

Unity

I

Heart of my heart, the world is young;
　　Love lies hidden in every rose!
Every song that the skylark sung
　　Once, we thought, must come to a close:
Now we know the spirit of song,
　　Song that is merged in the chant of the whole,
Hand in hand as we wander along,
　　What should we doubt of the years that roll?

II

Heart of my heart, we cannot die!
　　Love triumphant in flower and tree,
Every life that laughs at the sky
　　Tells us nothing can cease to be:
One, we are one with a song to-day,
　　One with the clover that scents the wold,
One with the Unknown, far away,
　　One with the stars, when earth grows old.

III

Heart of my heart, we are one with the wind,
　　One with the clouds that are whirled o'er the
　　　　lea,
One in many, O broken and blind,
　　One as the waves are at one with the sea!
Ay! when life seems scattered apart,
　　Darkens, ends as a tale that is told,
One, we are one, O heart of my heart,
　　One, still one, while the world grows old.

A May-Day Carol

What is the loveliest light that Spring
   Rosily parting her robe of grey
Girdled with leaflet green, can fling
   Over the fields where her white feet stray?
What is the merriest promise of May
   Flung o'er the dew-drenched April flowers?
Tell me, you on the pear-tree spray—
   Carol of birds between the showers.

What can life at its lightest bring
   Better than this on its brightest day?
How should we fetter the white-throat's wing
   Wild with joy of its woodland way?
Sweet, should love for an hour delay,
   Swift, while the primrose-time is ours!
What is the lover's royallest lay?—
   Carol of birds between the showers.

What is the murmur of bees a-swing?
   What is the laugh of a child at play?
What is the song that the angels sing?
   (Where were the tune could the sweet notes
     stay
Longer than this, to kiss and betray?)
   Nay, on the blue sky's topmost towers,
What is the song of the scraphim? Say—
   Carol of birds between the showers.

Thread the stars on a silver string,
  (So did they sing in Bethlehem's bowers!)
Mirth for a little one, grief for a king,
  Carol of birds between the showers.

Lavender

Lavender, lavender
  That makes your linen sweet;
The hawker brings his basket
  Down the sooty street:
The dirty doors and pavements
  Are simmering in the heat:
He brings a dream to London,
  And drags his weary feet.

Lavender, lavender,
  From where the bee hums,
To the loud roar of London,
  With purple dreams he comes,
From raggèd lanes of wild-flowers
  To raggèd London slums,
With a basket full of lavender
  And purple dreams he comes.

Is it nought to you that hear him?
  With the old strange cry
The weary hawker passes,
  And some will come and buy,
And some will let him pass away
  And only heave a sigh,

But most will neither heed nor hear
   When dreams go by.

Lavender, lavender!
   His songs were fair and sweet,
He brought us harvests out of heaven,
   Full sheaves of radiant wheat;
He brought us keys to Paradise,
   And hawked them thro' the street;
He brought his dreams to London,
   And dragged his weary feet.

Lavender, lavender!
   He is gone. The sunset glows;
But through the brain of London
   The mystic fragrance flows.
Each foggy cell remembers,
   Each raggèd alley knows,
The land he left behind him,
   The land to which he goes.

Poems by *William Carlos Williams*

This Is Just to Say

I have eaten
the plums
that were in
the icebox

and which
you were probably
saving
for breakfast

Forgive me
they were delicious
so sweet
and so cold

The Widow's Lament
in Springtime

Sorrow is my own yard
where the new grass
flames as it has flamed
often before but not
with the cold fire
that closes round me this year.
Thirtyfive years
I lived with my husband.

The plumtree is white today
with masses of flowers.
Masses of flowers
load the cherry branches
and color some bushes
yellow and some red
but the grief in my heart
is stronger than they
for though they were my joy
formerly, today I notice them
and turned away forgetting.
Today my son told me
that in the meadows,
at the edge of the heavy woods
in the distance, he saw
trees of white flowers.
I feel that I would like
to go there
and fall into those flowers
and sink into the marsh near them.

Poems by
Rupert Brooke

Pine-Trees and the Sky: Evening

I'd watched the sorrow of the evening sky,
And smelt the sea, and earth, and the warm
    clover,
And heard the waves, and the seagull's mocking
    cry.

And in them all was only the old cry,
That song they always sing—"The best is over!
You may remember now, and think, and sigh,
O silly lover!"
And I was tired and sick that all was over,
And because I,
For all my thinking, never could recover
One moment of the good hours that were over.
And I was sorry and sick, and wished to die.

Then from the sad west turning wearily,
I saw the pines against the white north sky.
Very beautiful, and still, and bending over
Their sharp black heads against a quiet sky.
And there was peace in them; and I
Was happy, and forgot to play the lover,
And laughed, and did no longer wish to die;
Being glad of you, O pine-trees and the sky!

Heaven

Fish (fly-replete, in depth of June,
Dawdling away their wat'ry noon)
Ponder deep wisdom, dark or clear,
Each secret fishy hope or fear.
Fish say, they have their Stream and Pond;
But is there anything Beyond?
This life cannot be All, they swear,
For how unpleasant, if it were!
One may not doubt that, somehow, Good
Shall come of Water and of Mud;
And, sure, the reverent eye must see
A Purpose in Liquidity.
We darkly know, by Faith we cry,
The future is not Wholly Dry.
Mud unto mud!—Death eddies near—
Not here the appointed End, not here!
But somewhere, beyond Space and Time.
Is wetter water, slimier slime!
And there (they trust) there swimmeth One
Who swam ere rivers were begun,
Immense, of fishy form and mind,
Squamous, omnipotent, and kind;
And under that Almighty Fin,
The littlest fish may enter in.
Oh! never fly conceals a hook,
Fish say, in the Eternal Brook,
But more than mundane weeds are there,
And mud, celestially fair;
Fat caterpillars drift around,
And Paradisal grubs are found;

Unfading moths, immortal flies,
And the worm that never dies.
And in that Heaven of all their wish,
There shall be no more land, say fish.

A Memory

Somewhile before the dawn I rose, and
    stept
  Softly along the dim way to your room,
  And found you sleeping in the quiet
    gloom,
And holiness about you as you slept.
I knelt there; till your waking fingers crept
  About my head, and held it. I had rest
  Unhoped this side of Heaven, beneath
    your breast.
I knelt a long time, still; nor even wept.

It was great wrong you did me; and for
    gain
Of that poor moment's kindliness, and
    ease,
And sleepy mother-comfort!
                        Child, you know
How easily love leaps out to dreams like
    these,
Who has seen them true. And love that's
    wakened so
Takes all too long to lay asleep again.

Song

"Oh! Love," they said, "is King of Kings,
    And Triumph is his crown.
Earth fades in flame before his wings,
    And Sun and Moon bow down."—
But that, I knew, would never do;
    And Heaven is all too high.
So whenever I met a Queen, I said,
    I will not catch her eye.

"Oh! Love," they said, and "Love," they said,
    "The gift of Love is this;
A crown of thorns about thy head,
    And vinegar to thy kiss!"—
But Tragedy is not for me;
    And I'm content to be gay.
So whenever I spied a Tragic Lady,
    I went another way.

And so I never feared to see
    You wander down the street,
Or come across the fields to me
    On ordinary feet.
For what they'd never told me of,
    And what I never knew;
It was that all the time, my love,
    Love would be merely you.

Dining-Room Tea

When you were there, and you, and you,
Happiness crowned the night; I too,
Laughing and looking, one of all,
I watched the quivering lamplight fall
On plate and flowers and pouring tea
And cup and cloth; and they and we
Flung all the dancing moments by
With jest and glitter. Lip and eye
Flashed on the glory, shone and cried,
Improvident, unmemoried;
And fitfully and like a flame
The light of laughter went and came.
Proud in their careless transience moved
The changing faces that I loved.

Till suddenly, and otherwhence,
I looked upon your innocence.
For lifted clear and still and strange
From the dark woven flow of change
Under a vast and starless sky
I saw the immortal moment lie.
One instant I, an instant, knew
As God knows all. And it and you
I, above Time, oh, blind! could see
In witless immortality.

I saw the marble cup; the tea,
Hung on the air, an amber stream;
I saw the fire's unglittering gleam,
The painted flame, the frozen smoke.

No more the flooding lamplight broke
On flying eyes and lips and hair;
But lay, but slept unbroken there,
On stiller flesh, and body breathless,
And lips and laughter stayed and deathless,
And words on which no silence grew.
Light was more alive than you.

For suddenly, and otherwhence,
I looked on your magnificence.
I saw the stillness and the light,
And you, august, immortal, white,
Holy and strange; and every glint
Posture and jest and thought and tint
Freed from the mask of transiency,
Triumphant in eternity,
Immote, immortal.

                   Dazed at length
Human eyes grew, mortal strength
Wearied; and Time began to creep.
Change closed about me like a sleep.
Light glinted on the eyes I loved.
The cup was filled. The bodies moved.
The drifting petal came to ground.
The laughter chimed its perfect round.
The broken syllable was ended.
And I, so certain and so friended,
How could I cloud, or how distress,
The heaven of your unconsciousness?
Or shake at Time's sufficient spell,
Stammering of lights unutterable?

The eternal holiness of you,
The timeless end, you never knew,
The peace that lay, the light that shone.
You never knew that I had gone
A million miles away, and stayed
A million years. The laughter played
Unbroken round me; and the jest
Flashed on. And we that knew the best
Down wonderful hours grew happier yet.
I sang at heart, and talked, and ate,
And lived from laugh to laugh, I too,
When you were there, and you, and you.

The Old Vicarage, Grantchester

(Café des Westens, Berlin, May, 1912)

Just now the lilac is in bloom,
All before my little room;
And in my flower-beds, I think,
Smile the carnation and the pink;
And down the borders, well I know,
The poppy and the pansy blow . . .
Oh! there the chestnuts, summer through,
Beside the river make for you
A tunnel of green gloom, and sleep
Deeply above; and green and deep
The stream mysterious glides beneath,
Green as a dream and deep as death.
—Oh, damn! I know it! and I know
How the May fields all golden show,

369

And when the day is young and sweet,
Gild gloriously the bare feet
That run to bathe . . .
                    Du lieber Gott!

Here am I, sweating, sick, and hot,
And there the shadowed waters fresh
Lean up to embrace the naked flesh.
Temperamentvoll German Jews
Drink beer around;—and *there* the dews
Are soft beneath a morn of gold.
Here tulips bloom as they are told;
Unkempt about those hedges blows
An English unofficial rose;
And there the unregulated sun
Slopes down to rest when day is done,
And wakes a vague unpunctual star,
A slippered Hesper; and there are
Meads towards Haslingfield and Coton
Where *das Betreten's* not *verboten.*

ἐλθε γενοίμην . . . would I were
In Grantchester, in Grantchester!—
Some, it may be, can get in touch
With Nature there, or Earth, or such.
And clever modern men have seen
A Faun a-peeping through the green,
And felt the Classics were not dead,
To glimpse a Naiad's reedy head,
Or hear the Goat-foot piping low: . . .
But these are things I do not know.
I only know that you may lie

Day long and watch the Cambridge sky,
And, flower-lulled in sleepy grass,
Hear the cool lapse of hours pass,
Until the centuries blend and blur
In Grantchester, in Grantchester. . . .
Still in the dawnlit waters cool
His ghostly Lordship swims his pool,
And tries the strokes, essays the tricks,
Long learnt on Hellespont, or Styx.
Dan Chaucer hears his river still
Chatter beneath a phantom mill.
Tennyson notes, with studious eye,
How Cambridge waters hurry by . . .
And in that garden, black and white,
Creep whispers through the grass all night;
And spectral dance, before the dawn,
A hundred Vicars down the lawn;
Curates, long dust, will come and go
On lissom, clerical, printless toe;
And oft between the boughs is seen
The sly shade of a Rural Dean . . .
Till, at a shiver in the skies,
Vanishing the Satanic cries,
The prim ecclesiastic rout
Leaves but a startled sleeper-out,
Grey heavens, the first bird's drowsy calls,
The falling house that never falls.

God! I will pack, and take a train,
And get me to England once again!
For England's the one land, I know,
Where men with Splendid Hearts may go;

And Cambridgeshire, of all England,
The shire for Men who Understand;
And of *that* district I prefer
The lovely hamlet Grantchester.
For Cambridge people rarely smile,
Being urban, squat, and packed with guile;
And Royston men in the far South
Are black and fierce and strange of mouth;
At Over they fling oaths at one,
And worse than oaths at Trumpington,

And Ditton girls are mean and dirty,
And there's none in Harston under thirty,
And folks in Shelford and those parts
Have twisted lips and twisted hearts,
And Barton men make Cockney rhymes,
And Coton's full of nameless crimes,
And things are done you'd not believe
At Madingley on Christmas Eve.
Strong men have run for miles and miles,
When one from Cherry Hinton smiles;
Strong men have blanched, and shot their
    wives,
Rather than send them to St. Ives;
Strong men have cried like babes, bydam,
To hear what happened at Babraham.
But Grantchester! ah, Grantchester!
There's peace and holy quiet there,
Great clouds along pacific skies,
And men and women with straight eyes,
Lithe children lovelier than a dream,
A bosky wood, a slumbrous stream,

And little kindly winds that creep
Round twilight corners, half asleep.
In Grantchester their skins are white;
They bathe by day, they bathe by night;
The women there do all they ought;
The men observe the Rules of Thought.
They love the Good; they worship Truth;
They laugh uproariously in youth;
(And when they get to feeling old,
They up and shoot themselves, I'm told) . . .

Ah God! to see the branches stir
Across the moon at Grantchester!
To smell the thrilling-sweet and rotten
Unforgettable, unforgotten
River-smell, and hear the breeze
Sobbing in the little trees.
Say, do the elm-clumps greatly stand
Still guardians of that holy land?
The chestnuts shade, in reverend dream,
The yet unacademic stream?
Is dawn a secret shy and cold
Anadyomene, silver-gold?
And sunset still a golden sea
From Haslingfield to Madingley?
And after, ere the night is born,
Do hares come out about the corn?
Oh, is the water sweet and cool,
Gentle and brown, above the pool?
And laughs the immortal river still
Under the mill, under the mill?
Say, is there Beauty yet to find?

And Certainty? and Quiet kind?
Deep meadows yet, for to forget
The lies, and truths, and pain? . . . oh! yet
Stands the Church clock at ten to three?
And is there honey still for tea?

Home

I came back late and tired last night
    Into my little room,
To the long chair and the firelight
    And comfortable gloom.

But as I entered softly in
    I saw a woman there,
The line of neck and cheek and chin,
    The darkness of her hair,
The form of one I did not know
    Sitting in my chair.

I stood a moment fierce and still,
    Watching her neck and hair.
I made a step to her; and saw
    That there was no one there.

It was some trick of the firelight
    That made me see her there.
It was a chance of shade and light
    And the cushion in the chair.

Oh, all you happy over the earth,
    That night, how could I sleep?
I lay and watched the lonely gloom;
    And watched the moonlight creep
From wall to basin, round the room.
    All night I could not sleep.

Poems by
Marianne Moore

O To Be a Dragon

If I, like Solomon, . . .
could have my wish—

my wish . . . O to be a dragon,
a symbol of the power of Heaven—of silkworm
size or immense; at times invisible.
Felicitous phenomenon!

No Swan So Fine

"No water so still as the
    dead fountains of Versailles.   No swan,
with swart blind look askance
and gondoliering legs,   so fine
    as the chintz china one with fawn-
brown eyes and toothed gold
collar on to show whose bird it was.

Lodged in the Louis Fifteenth
    candelabrum-tree   of cockscomb-
tinted buttons, dahlias,
sea-urchins, and everlastings,
    it perches on the branching foam
of polished sculptured
flowers—at ease and tall. The king is dead.

Poems by
T. S. Eliot

The Naming of Cats

The Naming of Cats is a difficult matter,
  It isn't just one of your holiday games;
You may think at first I'm as mad as a hatter
When I tell you, a cat must have THREE
    DIFFERENT NAMES.
First of all, there's the name that the family use
    daily,
  Such as Peter, Augustus, Alonzo or James,
Such as Victor or Jonathan, George or Bill
    Bailey—
  All of them sensible everyday names.
There are fancier names if you think they sound
    sweeter,
  Some for the gentlemen, some for the dames:
Such as Plato, Admetus, Electra, Demeter—
  But all of them sensible everyday names.
But I tell you, a cat needs a name that's
    particular,
  A name that's peculiar, and more dignified,
Else how can he keep up his tail perpendicular,
  Or spread out his whiskers, or cherish his
    pride?
Of names of this kind, I can give you a
    quorum,
  Such as Munkustrap, Quaxo, or Coricopat,
Such as Bombalurina, or else Jellylorum—
  Names that never belong to more than one cat.

But above and beyond there's still one name left
      over,
   And that is the name that you never will
      guess;
The name that no human research can
      discover—
   But THE CAT HIMSELF KNOWS, and will never
      confess.
When you notice a cat in profound meditation,
   The reason, I tell you, is always the same:
His mind is engaged in a rapt contemplation
   Of the thought, of the thought, of the
      thought of his name:
         His ineffable effable
         Effanineffable
Deep and inscrutable singular Name.

The Old Gumbie Cat

I have a Gumbie Cat in mind, her name is
      Jennyanydots;
Her coat is of the tabby kind, with tiger stripes
      and leopard spots.
All day she sits upon the stair or on the steps or
      on the mat;
She sits and sits and sits and sits—and that's
      what makes a Gumbie Cat!

   But when the day's hustle and bustle is done,
   Then the Gumbie Cat's work is but hardly
      begun.

And when all the family's in bed and asleep,
She tucks up her skirts to the basement to
  creep.
She is deeply concerned with the ways of the
  mice—
Their behaviour's not good and their manners
  not nice;
So when she has got them lined up on the
  matting,
She teaches them music, crocheting and
  tatting.

I have a Gumbie Cat in mind, her name is
  Jennyanydots;
Her equal would be hard to find, she likes the
  warm and sunny spots.
All day she sits beside the hearth or on the bed
  or on my hat:
She sits and sits and sits and sits—and that's
  what makes a Gumbie Cat!

But when the day's hustle and bustle is done,
Then the Gumbie Cat's work is but hardly
  begun.
As she finds that the mice will not ever keep
  quiet,
She is sure it is due to irregular diet;
And believing that nothing is done without
  trying,
She sets right to work with her baking and
  frying.

She makes them a mouse-cake of bread and
    dried peas,
And a *beautiful* fry of lean bacon and cheese.

I have a Gumbie Cat in mind, her name is
    Jennyanydots;
The curtain-cord she likes to wind, and tie it
    into sailor-knots.
She sits upon the window-sill, or anything that's
    smooth and flat:
She sits and sits and sits and sits—and that's
    what makes a Gumbie Cat!

But when the day's hustle and bustle is done,
Then the Gumbie Cat's work is but hardly
    begun.
She thinks that the cockroaches just need
    employment
To prevent them from idle and wanton
    destroyment.
So she's formed, from that lot of disorderly
    louts,
A troop of well-disciplined helpful boy-scouts,
With a purpose in life and a good deed to
    do—
And she's even created a Beetles' Tattoo.

So for Old Gumbie Cats let us now give three
    cheers—
On whom well-ordered households depend, it
    appears.

The Ad-dressing of Cats

You've read of several kinds of Cat,
And my opinion now is that
You should need no interpreter
To understand their character.
You now have learned enough to see
That Cats are much like you and me
And other people whom we find
Possessed of various types of mind.
For some are sane and some are mad
And some are good and some are bad
And some are better, some are worse—
But all may be described in verse.
You've seen them both at work and games,
And learnt about their proper names,
Their habits and their habitat:
But
    How would you ad-dress a Cat?

  So first, your memory I'll jog,
And say: A CAT IS NOT A DOG.

  Now dogs pretend they like to fight;
They often bark, more seldom bite;
But yet a Dog is, on the whole,
What you would call a simple soul.
Of course I'm not including Pekes,
And such fantastic canine freaks.
The usual Dog about the Town
Is much inclined to play the clown,
And far from showing too much pride

Is frequently undignified.
He's very easily taken in—
Just chuck him underneath the chin
Or slap his back or shake his paw,
And he will gambol and guffaw.
He's such an easy-going lout,
He'll answer any hail or shout.

Again I must remind you that
A Dog's a Dog—A CAT'S A CAT.

With Cats, some say, one rule is true:
Don't speak till you are spoken to.
Myself, I do not hold with that—
I say, you should ad-dress a Cat.
But always keep in mind that he
Resents familiarity.
I bow, and taking off my hat,
Ad-dress him in this form: O CAT!
But if he is the Cat next door,
Whom I have often met before
(He comes to see me in my flat)
I greet him with an OOPSA CAT!
I think I've heard them call him James—
But we've not got so far as names.
Before a Cat will condescend
To treat you as a trusted friend,
Some little token of esteem
Is needed, like a dish of cream;
And you might now and then supply
Some caviare, or Strassburg Pie,
Some potted grouse, or salmon paste—

He's sure to have his personal taste.
(I know a Cat, who makes a habit
Of eating nothing else but rabbit,
And when he's finished, licks his paws
So's not to waste the onion sauce.)
A Cat's entitled to expect
These evidences of respect.
And so in time you reach your aim,
And finally call him by his NAME.

So this is this, and that is that:
And there's how you AD-DRESS A CAT.

Poems by
Edna St. Vincent Millay

The Courage That My Mother Had

The courage that my mother had
Went with her, and is with her still:
Rock from New England quarried;
Now granite in a granite hill.

The golden brooch my mother wore
She left behind for me to wear;
I have no thing I treasure more:
Yet, it is something I could spare.

Oh, if instead she'd left to me
The thing she took into the grave!—
That courage like a rock, which she
Has no more need of, and I have.

The Buck in the Snow

White sky, over the hemlocks bowed with snow,
Saw you not at the beginning of evening the
  antlered buck and his doe
Standing in the apple-orchard? I saw them. I
  saw them suddenly go,
Tails up, with long leaps lovely and slow,
Over the stone-wall into the wood of hemlocks
  bowed with snow.

Now lies he here, his wild blood scalding the
  snow.

How strange a thing is death, bringing to his
  knees, bringing to his antlers
The buck in the snow.
How strange a thing,—a mile away by now, it
  may be,
Under the heavy hemlocks that as the moments
  pass
Shift their loads a little, letting fall a feather of
  snow—
Life, looking out attentive from the eyes of the
  doe.

From "Renascence"

All I could see from where I stood
Was three long mountains and a wood;
I turned and looked another way,
And saw three islands in a bay.
So with my eyes I traced the line
Of the horizon, thin and fine,
Straight around till I was come
Back to where I'd started from;
And all I saw from where I stood
Was three long mountains and a wood.

Over these things I could not see:
These were the things that bounded me.
And I could touch them with my hand,

Almost, I thought, from where I stand!
And all at once things seemed so small
My breath came short, and scarce at all.

But, sure, the sky is big, I said:
Miles and miles above my head.
So here upon my back I'll lie
And look my fill into the sky.
And so I looked, and after all,
The sky was not so very tall.
The sky, I said, must somewhere stop. . .
And—sure enough!—I see the top!
The sky, I thought, is not so grand;
I 'most could touch it with my hand!
And reaching up my hand to try,
I screamed, to feel it touch the sky.

I screamed, and—lo!—Infinity
Came down and settled over me;
Forced back my scream into my chest;
Bent back my arm upon my breast;
And, pressing of the Undefined
The definition on my mind,
Held up before my eyes a glass
Through which my shrinking sight did pass

Until it seemed I must behold
Immensity made manifold;
Whispered to me a word whose sound
Deafened the air for worlds around,

And brought unmuffled to my ears
The gossiping of friendly spheres,
The creaking of the tented sky,
The ticking of Eternity.

Poems by
e. e. cummings

O sweet spontaneous

O sweet spontaneous
earth how often have
the
doting

     fingers of
prurient philosophers pinched
and
poked

thee
, has the naughty thumb
of science prodded
thy

    beauty   . how
often have religions taken
thee upon their scraggy knees
squeezing and

buffeting thee that thou mightest conceive
gods
    (but
true

to the incomparable
couch of death thy

rhythmic
lover

   thou answerest

them only with

      spring)

when god lets my body be

when god lets my body be

From each brave eye shall sprout a tree
fruit that dangles therefrom

the purpled world will dance upon
Between my lips which did sing

a rose shall beget the spring
that maidens whom passion wastes

will lay between their little breasts
My strong fingers beneath the snow

Into strenuous birds shall go
my love walking in the grass

their wings will touch with her face
and all the while shall my heart be

With the bulge and nuzzle of the sea

Poems by
Ogden Nash

Complaint to
Four Angels

Every night at sleepy-time
Into bed I gladly climb.
Every night anew I hope
That with the covers I can cope.

Adjust the blanket fore and aft.
Swallow next a soothing draught;
Then a page of Scott or Cooper
May induce a healthful stupor.

O the soft luxurious dark,
Where carking cares no longer cark.
Traffic dies along the street.
The light is out. So are your feet.

Adjust the blanket aft and fore,
Sigh, and settle down once more.
Behold, a breeze! The curtains puff.
One blanket isn't quite enough.

Yawn and rise and seek your slippers,
Which, by now, are cold as kippers.
Yawn, and stretch, and prod yourself,
And fetch a blanket from the shelf.

And so to bed again, again,
Cozy under blankets twain.
Welcome warmth and sweet nirvana
Till eight o'clock or so mañana.

You sleep as deep as Crater Lake,
Then you dream and toss and wake.
Where is the breeze? There isn't any.
Two blankets, boy, are one too many.

O stilly night, why are you not
Consistent in your cold and hot?
O slumber's chains, unlocked so oft
With blankets being donned or doffed!

The angels who should guard my bed
I fear are slumbering instead.
O angels, please resume your hovering;
I'll sleep, and you adjust the covering.

Visitors Laugh at Locksmiths
or, Hospital Doors Haven't
Got Locks Anyhow

Something I should like to know is, which
    would everybody rather not do:
Be well and visit an unwell friend in the
    hospital, or be unwell in the hospital and
    have a well friend visit you?
Take the sight of a visitor trying to entertain a
    patient or a patient trying to entertain a visitor,

It would bring joy to the heart of the Grand
    Inquisitor.
The patient either is too ailing to talk or is
    panting to get back to the chapter where the
    elderly spinster is just about to reveal to the
    Inspector that she now thinks she can identify
    the second voice in that doom-drenched
    quarrel,
And the visitor either has never had anything to
    say to the patient anyway or is wondering
    how soon it would be all right to depart for
    Belmont or Santa Anita or Laurel,
And besides, even if both parties have ordinarily
    much to discuss and are far from
    conversational mediocrities,
Why, the austere hygienic surroundings and the
    lack of ashtrays would stunt a dialogue
    between Madame de Staël and Socrates,
And besides, even if anybody did get to chatting
    glitteringly and gaudily,
They would soon be interrupted by the arrival
    of a nurse or an orderly.
It is a fact that I must chronicle with distress
That the repartee reaches its climax when the
    visitor finally spots the handle on the foot of
    the bed and cranks the patient's knees up and
    down and says, That certainly is ingenious,
    and the patient answers Yes.
How many times a day do I finger my pulse and
    display my tongue to the mirror while waiting
    for the decision to jell:

405

Whether to ignore my host of disquieting symptoms and have to spend my days visiting friends who have surrendered to theirs, or to surrender to my own and spend my days being visited by friends who are thereby being punished for being well.

Poems by
Robert Penn Warren

Dragon-Tree

The faucet drips all night, the plumber forgot
    it.
A cat, in coitu, squalls like Hell's honeymoon.
A child is sick. The doctor coughs.
Do you feel, in your heart, that life has turned
    out as once you expected?

Spring comes early, ice
Groans in the gorge. Water, black, swirls
Into foam like lace white in fury. The gorge
    boulders boom.
When you hear, in darkness, the gorge boulders
    boom, does your heart say, "No comment"?

Geese pass in dawn-light, and the news
From Asia is bad, and the Belgians sure
    mucked up
The Congo. Human flesh is yet eaten there,
    often uncooked.
Have you sat on a hillside at sunset and eaten
    the flesh of your own heart?

The world drives at you like a locomotive
In an archaic movie. It whirls off the screen,
It is on you, the iron. You hear, in that silence,
    your heart.

Have you thought that the headlines are only
   the image of your own heart?

Some study compassion. Some, confusing
Personal pathology with the logic of history, jump
Out of windows. Some walk with God, some by
   rivers, at twilight.
Have you tried to just sit with the children and
   tell a tale ending in laughter?

Oh, tell the tale, and laugh, and let
God laugh—for your heart is the dragon-tree,
   the root
Feels, in earth-dark, the abrasive scale, the coils
Twitch. But look! the new leaf flaps gilt in the
   sunlight. Birds sing.

Ornithology in a World of Flux

It was only a bird call at evening, unidentified,
As I came from the spring with water, across
   the rocky back-pasture;
But so still I stood sky above was not stiller
   than sky in pail-water.

Years pass, all places and faces fade, some
   people have died,
And I stand in a far land, the evening still, and
   am at last sure
That I miss more that stillness at bird-call than
   some things that were to fail later.

410

Poems by
Louis MacNeice

Entirely

If we could get the hang of it entirely
 It would take too long;
All we know is the splash of words in passing
 And falling twigs of song,
And when we try to eavesdrop on the great
 Presences it is rarely
That by a stroke of luck we can appropriate
 Even a phrase entirely.

If we could find our happiness entirely
 In somebody else's arms
We should not fear the spears of the spring nor
  the city's
 Yammering fire alarms
But, as it is, the spears each year go through
 Our flesh and almost hourly
Bell or siren banishes the blue
 Eyes of Love entirely.

And if the world were black or white entirely
 And all the charts were plain
Instead of a mad weir of tigerish waters,
 A prism of delight and pain,
We might be surer where we wished to go
 Or again we might be merely
Bored but in brute reality there is no
 Road that is right entirely.

413

The Sunlight on the Garden

The sunlight on the garden
Hardens and grows cold,
We cannot cage the minute
Within its nets of gold,
When all is told
We cannot beg for pardon.

Our freedom as free lances
Advances towards its end;
The earth compels, upon it
Sonnets and birds descend;
And soon, my friend,
We shall have no time for dances.

The sky was good for flying
Defying the church bells
And every evil iron
Siren and what it tells:
The earth compels,
We are dying, Egypt, dying

And not expecting pardon,
Hardened in heart anew,
But glad to have sat under
Thunder and rain with you,
And grateful too
For sunlight on the garden.

Poems by
Theodore Roethke

The Waking

I wake to sleep, and take my waking slow.
I feel my fate in what I cannot fear.
I learn by going where I have to go.

We think by feeling. What is there to know?
I hear my being dance from ear to ear.
I wake to sleep, and take my waking slow.

Of those so close beside me, which are you?
God bless the Ground! I shall walk softly there,
And learn by going where I have to go.

Light takes the Tree; but who can tell us how?
The lowly worm climbs up a winding stair;
I wake to sleep, and take my waking slow.

Great Nature has another thing to do
To you and me; so take the lively air,
And, lovely, learn by going where to go.

This shaking keeps me steady. I should know.
What falls away is always. And is near.
I wake to sleep, and take my waking slow.
I learn by going where I have to go.

I Knew a Woman

I knew a woman, lovely in her bones,
When small birds sighed, she would sigh back
   at them;
Ah, when she moved, she moved more ways
   than one:
The shapes a bright container can contain!
Of her choice virtues only gods should speak,
Or English poets who grew up on Greek
(I'd have them sing in chorus, cheek to cheek).

How well her wishes went! She stroked my
   chin,
She taught me Turn, and Counter-turn, and
   Stand;
She taught me Touch, that undulant white skin;
I nibbled meekly from her proffered hand;
She was the sickle; I, poor I, the rake,
Coming behind her for her pretty sake
(But what prodigious mowing we did make).

Love likes a gander, and adores a goose:
Her full lips pursed, the errant note to seize;
She played it quick, she played it light and
   loose,
My eyes, they dazzled at her flowing knees;
Her several parts could keep a pure repose,
Or one hip quiver with a mobile nose
(She moved in circles, and those circles moved).

Let seed be grass, and grass turn into hay:
I'm martyr to a motion not my own;
What's freedom for? To know eternity.
I swear she cast a shadow white as stone.
But who would count eternity in days?
These old bones live to learn her wanton ways:
(I measure time by how a body sways).

Poems by
Elizabeth Bishop

Sestina

September rain falls on the house.
In the failing light, the old grandmother
sits in the kitchen with the child
beside the Little Marvel Stove,
reading the jokes from the almanac,
laughing and talking to hide her tears.

She thinks that her equinoctial tears
and the rain that beats on the roof of the house
were both foretold by the almanac,
but only known to a grandmother.
The iron kettle sings on the stove.
She cuts some bread and says to the child,

It's time for tea now; but the child
is watching the teakettle's small hard tears
dance like mad on the hot black stove,
the way the rain must dance on the house.
Tidying up, the old grandmother
hangs up the clever almanac

on its string. Birdlike, the almanac
hovers half open above the child,
hovers above the old grandmother
and her teacup full of dark brown tears.
She shivers and says she thinks the house
feels chilly, and puts more wood in the stove.

It was to be, says the Marvel Stove.
I know what I know, says the almanac.
With crayons the child draws a rigid house
and a winding pathway. Then the child
puts in a man with buttons like tears
and shows it proudly to the grandmother.

But secretly, while the grandmother
busies herself about the stove,
the little moons fall down like tears
from between the pages of the almanac
into the flower bed the child
has carefully placed in the front of the house.

Time to plant tears, says the almanac.
The grandmother sings to the marvellous stove
and the child draws another inscrutable house.

One Art

The art of losing isn't hard to master;
so many things seem filled with the intent
to be lost that their loss is no disaster.

Lose something every day. Accept the fluster
of lost door keys, the hour badly spent.
The art of losing isn't hard to master.

Then practice losing farther, losing faster:
places, and names, and where it was you meant
to travel. None of these will bring disaster.

I lost my mother's watch. And look! my last, or
next-to-last, of three loved houses went.
The art of losing isn't hard to master.

I lost two cities, lovely ones. And, vaster,
some realms I owned, two rivers, a continent.
I miss them, but it wasn't a disaster.

—Even losing you (the joking voice, a gesture
I love) I shan't have lied. It's evident
the art of losing's not too hard to master
though it may look like (*Write* it!) like disaster.

Poems by
Robert Lowell

Skunk Hour

(FOR ELIZABETH BISHOP)

Nautilus Island's hermit
heiress still lives through winter in her Spartan
   cottage;
her sheep still graze above the sea.
Her son's a bishop. Her farmer
is first selectman in our village;
she's in her dotage.

Thirsting for
the hierarchic privacy
of Queen Victoria's century,
she buys up all
the eyesores facing her shore,
and lets them fall.

The season's ill—
we've lost our summer millionaire,
who seemed to leap from an L. L. Bean
catalogue. His nine-knot yawl
was auctioned off to lobstermen.
A red fox stain covers Blue Hill.

And now our fairy
decorator brightens his shop for fall;
his fishnet's filled with orange cork,

orange, his cobbler's bench and awl;
there is no money in his work,
he'd rather marry.

One dark night,
my Tudor Ford climbed the hill's skull;
I watched for love-cars. Lights turned down,
they lay together, hull to hull,
where the graveyard shelves on the town. . . .
My mind's not right.

A car radio bleats,
"Love, O careless Love. . . ." I hear
my ill-spirit sob in each blood cell,
as if my hand were at its throat. . . .
I myself am hell;
nobody's here—

only skunks, that search
in the moonlight for a bite to eat.
They march on their soles up Main Street:
white stripes, moonstruck eyes' red fire
under the chalk-dry and spar spire
of the Trinitarian Church.

I stand on top
of our back steps and breathe the rich air—
a mother skunk with her column of kittens
    swills the garbage pail.
She jabs her wedge-head in a cup
of sour cream, drops her ostrich tail,
and will not scare.

Water

It was a Maine lobster town—
each morning boatloads of hands
pushed off for granite
quarries on the islands,

and left dozens of bleak
white frame houses stuck
like oyster shells
on a hill of rock,

and below us, the sea lapped
the raw little match-stick
mazes of a weir,
where the fish for bait were trapped.

Remember? We sat on a slab of rock.
From this dance in time,
it seems the color
of iris, rotting and turning purpler,

but it was only
the usual gray rock
turning the usual green
when drenched by the sea.

The sea drenched the rock
at our feet all day,
and kept tearing away
flake after flake.

One night you dreamed
you were a mermaid clinging to a wharf-pile,
and trying to pull
off the barnacles with your hands.

We wished our two souls
might return like gulls
to the rock. In the end,
the water was too cold for us.

INDEX OF TITLES

435

Surprised by Joy   77

INDEX OF AUTHORS

INDEX OF FIRST LINES

443